The Write Spot: Musings and Ravings From a Pandemic Year

Praise for
The Write Spot: Musings and Ravings From a Pandemic Year

Upheaval in our lives around the world in 2020—who knew? Marlene Cullen's seventh edition of The Write Spot anthologies seizes this tumultuous year to focus on writers' experiences that reflect many of our own as we stumbled along in this new rhythm in our era of COVID. From a sudden new vocabulary having become our overnight norm, (Zoom, COVID), we find common ground in these newfound reflections.

So much togetherness leads one writer to glory in a "fifteen-minute shower alone [that] feels like a solo weekend getaway," while another realizes an individual introspective moment "is not a monologue but actually a dialogue."

What we thought was a vacuum can actually be "empty spaces that define what's there." Aside from what we learn about ourselves, memories provide some levity as one writer paints herself with amazing clarity, stating "what I won't tell you," while a vignette of a kleptomaniac cat's penchant to abscond with puzzle pieces ironically solves the last piece of a missing puzzle.

But while one writer's memory harkens back to pre-COVID times and a distasteful episode as she worked as a waitress, we remember that we still have much to overcome, COVID and more.

—Janis Couvreux, *Sail Cowabunga!*

Award winning author of *Sail Cowabunga! A Family's 10 Years at Sea,* Janis Couvreux is a journalist, sailor, mom, grandmom, traveler, and Franco-American, and has blogged at *The Huffington Post* and The Lady Alliance about living bilingually, crossing oceans, backpacking adventures, and raising kids outside the box.

What I appreciate most about *The Write Spot: Musings and Ravings From a Pandemic Year* is its cornucopia of honest exploration into the human condition during, but not exclusive to the COVID-era. Nature as nurturer is interwoven in this lively collection that is filled with wisdom, prompts, and inspiration for those seeking the lift of a literary life.

I savored the seamless connection between these wonderful, honest writers in one sitting, a mug of tea in hand. Writers need other writers to remind us why we do what we do.

It is the subtle evolution of our everyday ideals that help us see the patterns emerging in the space between each writer's words.

This book is a timely reminder of how busy we've all been while stuck at home, striving to uncover that elusive state of grace buried within the fog of a pandemic.

—Frances Rivetti

Frances Rivetti is an award-winning British/American journalist and author of *Fog Valley Crush—Love at First Bite* and *Fog Valley Winter—Pioneer Heritage, Backroad Rambles and Vintage Recipes,* and a novel, *Big Green Country.* Her articles have been published in print and online in the UK, Australia, and the United States. She lives in Sonoma County, Northern California.

The Write Spot founder and writing coach Marlene Cullen has been guiding writers through her Jumpstart workshops. I've been lucky to participate in some of them. Marlene's motto is "just write," as in don't stop to evaluate what you've written during the drafting process—just keep the pen moving until the timer rings. In this collection, she has gathered a wide variety of poetry and short prose pieces from sixteen writers.

If there's a common thread that binds this anthology, it's grappling with the surreal nature of 2020 and the coronavirus pandemic. Being forced to upend our "normal" lives and adapt to changing threats, both medical and socio-political, has created an opportunity for deep investigation that finds catharsis, much-needed humor, and rich forays into family memories.

There are inviting dips into the pool of childhood experience, replete with first kisses, chaperoned high school dances, the veneer of the perfect family, and the truth behind that veneer, like a skinned knee that's lost its bandage.

The saga of battling a feisty garden raccoon had me laughing out loud. By turns moving, poignant, funny, and wistful, the pieces in this collection are redolent with sensory detail, the smells of everyday life, and sounds that root us to places and memories, such as the music of crickets on summer nights.

Life's passages are celebrated through generational connections between friends and family, love, death and birth. This collection balances the specifics of our individual lives with a sense of universality.

The Write Spot: Musings and Ravings From a Pandemic Year is a treasure and not to be missed.

—Sandra Anfang

Sandra Anfang is a poet, teacher, and artist who lives in the California wine country north of San Francisco. She teaches poetry writing to students from elementary through high school. Her poetry collections include *Looking Glass Heart* (Finishing Line Press, 2016), *Road Worrier: Poems of the Inner and Outer Landscape* (Finishing Line Press, 2018), and *Xylem Highway* (Main Street Rag, 2019). To write, for her, is to breathe. Visit her at sandeanfangart.com

Also Available in The Write Spot Series

The Write Spot to Jumpstart Your Writing: Discoveries

Shares techniques used in Jumpstart Writing Workshops.

"Reading this anthology is like walking into a word bazaar, where the reader is called to taste grief's shadows, to sample sweet memories. The reader is beckoned by the poetry of human existence, lured to the scents and sounds of places and times. Savor this visit to worlds familiar and unfamiliar. You will leave, feeling satisfied."

—Claudia Larson

The Write Spot to Jumpstart Your Writing: Connections

Writing from mothers and their children illustrate how we relate through stories.

"Heartfelt conviction, strong imagery, and the generational connections make the pieces in Marlene Cullen's *The Write Spot to Jumpstart Your Writing: Connections* an excellent anthology of mini-memoirs. The book is a powerful testament to the way the written word connects and inspires us. The prompts will help you write your own stories."

—B. Lynn Goodwin, WriterAdvice
and author of *Never Too Late* and *Talent*

The Write Spot: Reflections

A treasure chest of anecdotes, vignettes, and poems.

"To see the world in a grain of sand or the future in a ball of lightning, to see meanings in a psychedelic bubble or in a glass bottle of Coca-Cola, *Reflections* vividly mirrors elements of our multifaceted lives—imagined by a myriad of sharp-eyed writers. This anthology brings the everyday into focus with a brightness of spirit that we all can admire, and be inspired!"

—Kate F.

The Write Spot: Memories

Diverse narratives from fathers and their children embrace a common thread of love, disappointment, discoveries, and revelations.

"Marlene Cullen's collection of short essays compiled in *The Write Spot: Memories* unfolds like a gently-made, multicolored origami box. Each story is its own piece, its own regretful, loving, confusing, humorous, illuminating tale, yet held together by one theme that touches us all—our fathers and our memories of them when we were children, and our awakenings about them as we became adults. *Memories* is for anyone who has had a father whether present or absent, loving or distant, authoritarian or goofball. Authentic and relatable, each story is written with deep insight and love."

—Julie

The Write Spot: Possibilities

A mixture of playful, experimental, insightful stories as well as prompts and resources for writers.

"These words will touch your heart and might even move your pen."

—Brenda Bellinger, author of *Taking Root*

The Write Spot: Writing as a Path to Healing

Illustrates how to write about difficult topics without adding trauma.

"Quite possibly the most deeply moving volume in the Write Spot series. The contributing writers delve into the pain of their past, reveal their vulnerabilities, and share the lessons they've learned. Their courage is written on every page of this collection.

"Even while she's editing an anthology, Cullen has her mind on writers. She understands that writing through difficult life events can unearth strong emotions and memories and so she includes resources for the writer's mental and emotional support—and that's what makes the Write Spot series more than just a collection of stories."

—Elizabeth Beechwood

The Write Spot

Musings and Ravings From a Pandemic Year

—Book 7 in The Write Spot Series—

Spring 2021

Marlene Cullen, Editor

The Write Spot: Musings and Ravings From a Pandemic Year

Book 7 in The Write Spot Series

ISBN: 978-1-941066-62-1

Book design by Jo-Anne Rosen
Cover design by Judy Baker

M. Cullen Enterprises
Petaluma, California
an imprint of Wordrunner Press

Winter Solstice 2020

M.A. Dooley

To re-build beauty we split the wood
Don't split the hairs, it does no good

To build more beauty, we light the flame
The kindling catches, we say the names

Of those we love who went beyond
They shaped our lives, they're never gone

Reflection first, then put it away
Forgive, don't forget, make up one day

Let go the work, the world of greed
The rules of day, the ego needs

Gathered in darkness wait for the light
Beauty glows on faces this firelit night

The circle round holds hearts and dreams,
Tears fall for loves no longer seen

The year was wrought with judging and pain
Hindsight 2020 the last refrain

Awake on the longest night, the fire
Releases suffering and unmet desires

This invocation is for you,
You represent your sisters too

For mothers, daughters we hold you dear
For fathers, sons not shaped by fear

We stand for sacredness of life, for living
The year's behind us without misgiving

We stand together and hold our place
Embrace salvation of the human race

We are so close to being one
Let's end this year with love and fun.

Humor

Karen Handyside Ely

When the day is dark
humor will light my way.

When the world crumbles
humor will shore me up.

Tears will flow, not from sorrow,
but born of laugher.

Nothing is so bad that
humor cannot soften it.

Nothing is so sacred that
humor cannot humanize it.

When the only way through
is a walk of fire,

humor will insulate my path.
As long as we can laugh

at the absurdities of life,
we can persevere.

Humor cannot change our challenges,
but it can grease the skids,

shepherd us along,
help us to survive.

I will face each day with humor and the grace it provides.
As long as I can laugh, I can breathe.

Humor is my lifeboat,
my safe space.

Humor is the fuel my soul feeds on.

Contents

Introduction

On March 19, 2020 when the order was given to shelter in place in California, I thought we would be confined for one or two months. I had been following my friend's journey in Italy with their mandates of staying home and wearing masks when going out. That sounded extreme. I saw photos of empty streets in Florence where she lived and thought that will never happen here.

But, of course, it did happen here. Navigating the maze of staying safe became a world-wide endeavor.

Less than a month after the shelter in place order, I realized the importance of documenting thoughts and emotions, like a snapshot or a still life painting, chronicling this confusing chapter of our history. I wanted to know what writers were thinking during the surreal time from mid-March through December 2020.

The responses to my call for writing shaped this anthology; stories about survival techniques, masks as accessories, gardening as an instrument of grace.

Writers were willing to be vulnerable in telling their stories of finding ways to survive and manage both the pandemic and painful childhoods. They overcame lethargy and ennui to tell stories of loss, vintage treasures, being in nature, dance as therapy, and remembering fathers even when they were less than perfect.

One person wrote about the difficulties of being hard of hearing and how mask wearing makes it impossible to read lips. Emotional discoveries, stories of gratitude, and descriptions of relationships that can never be fixed are revealed with a behind-the-scenes feel of looking past the veneer.

I asked each contributor what energizes them. The answers illustrate the importance of self-care: walking, swimming, being in nature, accomplishing projects, imagining, dancing, meditating, and accepting what cannot be changed.

Some of the fiction, poetry, and creative non-fiction narratives in this anthology are serious, others are humorous. Many pieces were written from a desire for introspection and discovery.

It will be interesting to read what historians will say about this tumultuous year. For now, we can read what some writers were thinking and experiencing.

There are writing prompts to inspire your own writing. Some prompts are poignant, some invite summer memories, others list how to handle middle of the night anxieties—any of these prompts can be used to enrich your writing.

The list of recommended books includes how to write memoir, memoirs that can be used as textbooks, and books on writing you may have never heard of.

In a year that felt like a harrowing emotional roller coaster ride, I invite you to explore these pages and remember you aren't alone on this journey called Life.

Our pandemic year has been a challenge, a change, and an opportunity, all rolled together. Mask wearing, physical distancing, Zoom parties and events have become part of our "new normal."

My takeaway from 2020 is that it's important to connect. Phone a friend just to say hello. Write to explore your thoughts and feelings. Read inspirational stories.

Collect writing that calms and inspires, like M.A. Dooley's *Winter Solstice 2020* and Karen Handyside Ely's *Humor* to read and re-read when the journey is hard and it seems there is nothing to look forward to. Reading favorite pieces can restore the sense that everything will be okay.

And breathe. Remember to breathe.

What have you learned during shelter in place?

Marlene Cullen
January 2021

The Write Spot: Musings and Ravings From a Pandemic Year

Empty Desks

Before summer break, I watched our grandson squirming in his seat at home, laptop on the table in front of him, eagerly waiting to be "unmuted" by his kindergarten teacher so he could tell her about the quail we saw on our walk that morning. He was so excited to have found an animal whose name begins with the letter "Q."

Heading into August, I found myself thinking about how different this year's back-to-school ritual must seem to kids and their parents. Our local schools were planning to begin their fall classes with "distance learning," another new term to add to our growing pandemic lexicon. Teachers, in their empty classrooms, would be providing instruction through a video connection to students logged in at home. This presents so many challenges for everyone involved: teachers, working parents, families who lack connectivity and, most especially, the children.

I had posted these thoughts on my blog, along with a photo of a child's desk, vintage 1900, that was mine when I lived with my grandparents as a young child on the East Coast. The legs are cast iron and the top is covered in red leather with an inkwell.

I remember that desk being near my grandmother's kitchen where I could watch Nana while she cooked, and I colored. Or was she watching me? I drew so many pictures there—lots of houses that had two windows with four panes each, tied back curtains, red brick chimneys with curlicues of smoke billowing out and curved walkways leading to the front door.

When I was eight, my mother and I left that home and moved to the West Coast where she would marry the man who became my stepfather. The little desk stayed behind. In 1977, my grandmother died, two weeks before my first son was born. Three years later, my grandfather offered to have the desk crated and shipped to me in California by rail, thinking his great-grandson would enjoy it. I declined his kind offer, feeling sure the cost of shipping would far exceed the value of the desk. Several years later, I learned that my uncle had picked up the desk. He had no children but thought it would make a nice addition to his front porch in Rhode Island. My grandfather passed in 1983 and my uncle was named executor of his estate. Sadly, he died two years later, before the estate was settled. While the probate case slowly made its way through the local court, the desk became weathered. The iron legs were beginning to rust, and the leather had started to crack and peel.

Fast forward to Christmas Day, 1993. I arrived at my parents' home in Santa Rosa, California, bearing a large tray of homemade cookies I'd baked. I was about to set them down on the dining table for a moment when my dad pointed and said, "Put them over there." There it was. Right next to the kitchen. The desk had been completely and beautifully restored. It bore a gift tag that read, "To my kid. Love, Dad."

It's with me now, in my writing studio, right next to my big desk. My grandchildren use it sometimes when they visit, lifting the heavy lid to pull out paper, crayons, and pencils as I did all those years ago.

It survived. So will we.

Prompt: Write about a special gift.

My Wedgewood Stove

When my husband and I bought our property—an old chicken farm—back in the early 80s, the previous owners removed the electric range they'd bought for the kitchen and took it with them.

Duane rummaged around in the one chicken house that was still standing. The main house and mobile home had both been rentals for a while; long enough for the outbuildings (a warehouse and a Quonset hut) to fill up with an assortment of things abandoned or forgotten. One of these was a boat that had been carelessly backed into the chicken house where it destroyed one of the upright supports. That boat, owned by a long-deceased friend of the previous owner, is what has kept that section of the building from completely collapsing, to this day.

Duane found the Wedgewood gas stove in the chicken house. For me, it was love at first sight. We managed to get it into the kitchen where the gas connection lined up perfectly. The stove was returned to its original spot.

As near as we've been able to tell, the stove is vintage mid-40s. It has four stovetop burners, an oven with a broiler underneath, and to the left of the oven, a storage area for pots and pans. Two of the burners and the pilot in the oven must be lit manually each time. A cooking chart is still legible on the inside of the oven door with times and temperatures for things like sponge cake and "well larded" veal. I strike a match, lay it over the hole that says, "light here" and then turn on the gas. Voila!

Sunday breakfasts have always been my most favorite meal to cook. I remember one morning, when all four boys still lived at home. I laid the cast iron griddle across the two burners on the left side and was mixing pancake batter while cards were being dealt on the kitchen table behind me. Flipping pancakes, I suddenly wondered where the years had gone. This was the same stove, same kitchen where I'd warmed their baby bottles, baked cookies, and fixed their favorite meals. Now they were playing poker? And then, one by one, they were gone.

But it wasn't long before the stove was warming baby bottles, baking cookies, and turning out Sunday breakfasts again, this time for the grandchildren.

Now, it's just Duane and me for the most part. This stove, that is older than I am, still does everything I ask of it. In recent weeks, during the COVID-19 lockdown, it seems I've been cooking non-stop since we're not eating meals out at all. Tonight, that old stove and I will bake a loaf of banana bread.

Prompt: What do you love most about the place you call home?

The Power of Words—Writing Prompts for Difficult Times

What I need now are the words that I'm having trouble finding, the words that are buried deep below a lifetime of learned behaviors and measured responses.

What I wish I could say is that there is no more poverty in America, that homelessness has been eradicated, that everyone has equal opportunities in this country regardless of their skin color, that police in every jurisdiction believe their role is to serve and protect the rights of citizens while upholding the law.

It makes me uncomfortable, but my ear has now become finely tuned to the subtle nuances of racism expressed by some members of my family.

"Being the change I wish to see" means calling that out, raising my voice to challenge theirs, and refusing to be silent.

Taking a stand would look like walking the talk, demonstrating through my actions and my voice that my values are different than theirs.

The values I stand for are based on equality for everyone at every stage of Maslow's hierarchy of needs from the physiological basics of food, water, shelter, and health to safety and security, love and belonging, self-esteem and opportunities to reach self-actualization.

If I aligned my voice with my values, I would be marching shoulder-to-shoulder with others in protest, my voice joining theirs in demanding what is right and just and long overdue.

The person I want to be would be someone who could say she's proud to be an American.

Hearing the news, my heart asks "What have we become as a country?"

In my body right now, I feel ashamed to be white.

The saddest part for me on a personal level, is to realize that I'm somewhat envious of the passing of a friend in early April, who never had to know that a white police officer in Minneapolis would slowly, deliberately, and intentionally grind the life out of a Black man by shear physical force while other officers stood passively by and that this is only one of several such incidents nationwide.

Whatever I do, I must not let these words die in passivity on the page as merely arranged typographic letters offered in response to a prompt.

I am committed to listening, to paying attention, to challenging my assumptions, and not turning away, or hiding under my white skin—becoming complicit by my silence.

Making a difference means standing up for what you believe is right, calling out injustice, demanding accountability from those who govern and represent us, and applying the Golden Rule to everyone—every day.

Alongside the suffering, I also see a little Black girl comforted by a kneeling white officer who assures her that he is there to protect her and her parents during the protest. He tells her that she can march or even dance if she likes. And I see a young Black flight attendant unable to hold back her tears when a white middle-aged male passenger, reading "White Fragility" offers a heartfelt apology, saying "It's our fault."

What I want future generations to know is that this is where it begins. Where there is hope, there can be change.

We can't rewrite our shameful history, but we must not allow ourselves to be condemned to repeat it.

Prompts (in bold type) were provided by Kelly Notaras of KN Literary Arts to help us write through the difficult and transformative events including and following the killing of George Floyd in Minneapolis on May 25, 2020.

What energizes you?

A walk in the woods or on the beach.

As I write this, I'm recalling our last visit to old growth redwoods in Humboldt County. We can't travel north on Highway 101 without exiting to follow the Avenue of the Giants for a while, stopping here and there to walk along a duff path on the forest floor, under the protection of these majestic trees.

And the ocean! I swear I can walk all day along the water's edge, inches away from the reach of the waves, salt air filling my lungs, bits of tumbled sea glass and shells finding their way to my pockets. The sound of the ocean, like white noise, muffles everything but my thoughts.

Walking is always an energy booster for me whether alone or in the company of a friend. During the time two of our grandchildren lived with us, I'd walk them almost a mile to school every weekday morning at 7:45 as long as it was above forty degrees and not pouring down rain. A light drizzle wouldn't stop me, even if *they* protested. In Ireland, they call a light mist lovely soft weather. I agree.

A good walk, away from screens, chores, and disruptions, refreshes my body and mind leaving me ready to tackle whatever the day might put in front of me.

But first, coffee.

Brenda Bellinger

Transplanted from Connecticut to California as a young child, Brenda Bellinger has never forgotten her early years in New England. Now a Nana herself, she treasures opportunities to build memories with her grandchildren.

Brenda's work has appeared in *Small Farmer's Journal*, *Mom Egg Review*, *Persimmon Tree*, *THEMA*, *The California Writers Club Literary Review* and in various anthologies.

She has been honored with first place awards for nonfiction and flash fiction at the Mendocino Coast and Central Coast Writers Conferences, respectively.

Her first novel, *Taking Root,* a young adult story of betrayal and courage, is available on Amazon. Brenda blogs at brendabellinger.com.

A Little Sweetness

So many crises, one piled on another. How do I not sink under their weight?

I walk to the river almost every day, where I try to observe as much of nature as possible—birds, trees, gardens, the mood of the river's flow. All these take me away from the daily drumbeat of the news.

Yesterday I saw a night heron perched on a tree branch overhanging the water. He eyed me as I walked slowly by. I tried to reassure him I meant no harm. Just seeing him was a gift bestowed by the river.

Today an egret stood at attention on the far bank, ducks flew overhead, a crow in the street worked at cracking a walnut with his beak.

All these small details, these miracles of life around me, comfort me. Tomorrow, the next day and the day after, I hope to keep my eye on what is important to me. National and international events are important, not to be ignored, but within myself, I need a little sweetness to fight the bitterness.

Prompt: Yesterday: Today.

Evening Shadows

When evening shadows
dim the garden's glow
and rise to greet the night,
Nocturnal creatures tip-toe
to dine on leafy delight.

Till early morning's fingers
touch the edge of heaven's air,
fading darkness.
Warning.
Time to go.

Prompt: Windows.

Red

Growing up I was a tomboy, preferring tree climbing to dolls. I loved pretending to be a cowboy. Decked out in my cowboy hat, boots, holster, and gun, I could ride Red, my Shetland pony, off into the sunset like any of the TV cowboys I watched—Roy Rogers, Paladin, Matt Dillon.

I could make Red trot around our half-acre front yard chasing imaginary outlaws or Indians. Occasionally he bucked me off or tried to knock me off by passing under a low hanging branch, but if he succeeded, I just got back on like any good cowboy.

In summer I liked keeping a lookout in the apple tree watching for Indians or outlaws who might disturb the town, but I took a book along, knowing I wouldn't see anybody. Red grazed below on grass and fallen apples.

In winter when I couldn't ride Red, I joined him in the barn, turning over his oat pail for a seat, and told him about my day. He seemed to listen and nuzzled my hand in case I'd brought him a treat.

When I couldn't ride Red, I could still play at being a cowboy by setting up my ranch set with plastic horses and fences to corral them. Using cardboard from my father's laundered shirts, I constructed a frontier town, the saloon taking center stage with its swinging, half-door entrance like the one I'd seen on *Gunsmoke*. I didn't identify with Kitty, the saloon keeper. I couldn't imagine her riding a bareback horse as I sometimes did on little Red. I wanted to be Matt, the sheriff.

It was a sad day when I got too tall to ride little Red, but a happy one for him. My uncle had a Marine buddy who owned a farm and had three little girls. Red was going to a new home.

One Sunday, my father took the backseat out of the old Buick. Then with some difficulty, he and I loaded Red into the car. Red's head hung over the front seat between us as we started for the farm. Stopping for a signal on the way, the people in the car next to us noticed Red and pointed at us, laughing at the unusual sight.

We passed fields of ripening corn, grazing cows behind white fences and big red barns. Many narrow country lanes led to the farm where the farmer and his family came out to greet us. His wife and daughters, dressed in their Sunday best, didn't approach Red but couldn't take their eyes off him. The farmer led Red to a pasture full of cows where he opened the gate and turned Red loose. Red picked up his ears and trotted over to his new family.

I would miss him, but pretended otherwise, knowing this farm was a good home for him. No tears were shed. Cowboys don't cry.

Prompt: Pretending.

What energizes you?

If 2020 had been a normal year, a close friend and I would have traveled to Oxford and the Cotswolds of England.

My travel bug began in 1956 when my parents drove along Route 66 from Chicago to Los Angeles then up to San Francisco.

San Francisco enchanted me so much that, six years later I journeyed there via Greyhound bus to make it my home and attend college. Through the college's International Program, I studied in Sweden and explored more of Europe by train, boat, and hitchhiking.

During these past ten years, my travel has been on tours making logistics easier with well-informed guides and interesting fellow travelers. The first of these started in Paris, journeyed down to Nice, up through the wine country and north to Mont St. Michael and the beaches of the Normandy invasion of 1944. The next year started in London over to Wales, up to Hadrian's wall and ended in Bath. Then followed a more exotic tour to Istanbul with its ancient Greek, Roman and Byzantine history, beautiful Islamic mosques and the Aegean Sea.

Year after year we travelled. Thinking about future travel possibilities, seeing and learning about new places and meeting fellow-travelers, energizes me. Soon, in the not-too-distant future, my friend and I will be planning our next travel adventure.

In the meantime, there are quieter adventures here at home. Today it was a Great Blue Heron on the opposite bank of the local river and a flock of small shore birds flitting by like a passing cloud. Small adventures await, just a walk away.

Cheryl Moore

Cheryl Moore has been interested in nature since reading Little Golden Books about trees and birds in childhood through receiving a degree in biology.

When she lived in Tehran during the early 1970's, she managed a small research library where biologists studied the wildlife of Iran. When young animals were left parentless, the biologists often cared for them. One afternoon Cheryl babysat an Asiatic black bear cub in the library until a caregiver was found. Other youngsters she saw were three cheetah kittens, a wolf puppy, and a baby leopard, ferocious in its cage. She sometimes writes about this exotic time and place and marvels at how much the world has changed.

She lives in a house and garden where deer nibble on roses and tomato leaves and raccoons dine on fallen figs. She is lucky to have birds visit her feeders and a river nearby to walk where waterfowl abound. Seeing and writing about these miracles of nature bring her comfort during these trying times.

Black & White, Mussels & Fries

Mussels and fries
white wine
shallots and thyme
black and white
cement tiles
white apron with
long ties
black shells
piling on plates
white and steaming
behind the cook's
black hair
teased in a twist
French gone beehive
white skin black heels
white sandals scurrying
kitchen
bar and
dining areas
inside
outside
lunch and dinner
before sunset
June and July
long lazy busy days
depending
tourists and regulars

I cannot remember
her mind on naked feet
slicing waves
baring words
hitting nerves
too many to
trace and recount
17 wrapped
in the sleeveless sheath
of a green dress
I'd know these hips a mile away
he said
while she
though pleased
remained untouched
shrouded in fatherly words
yet not
unscathed
boss's friend's hand
patting her where
he shouldn't have
boss's laughter
sanctioning friend's gesture
her eyes aflame
anger and shame
standing scandal upon
black and white tiles
no ties
but a bow at
the back of a
white apron
no heels

naked feet in summer sandals
no right
but a black and blue
heart of pride
I quit
she said

Prompt: Write about a summer job.

The Grace of a Garden, May 2020

Gardening has been an instrument of grace while sheltering in place during the COVID-19 pandemic. The grounds around the house have never looked better maintained, by bohemian standards. We—my husband and I—even planted a few vegetables in the boxes between the lilac and fig trees, and converted an old rusty water heater split in halves into improvised cradles for the Japanese cucumber seedlings we bought during one of our risky forays into the world of Friedman's Home Improvement, where diligently masked customers waited in line obligingly six feet apart. Except for a trip out for groceries every ten days, we had not been out in six weeks. The nursery section of the store was a zoo, not so much the hardware side: no lines there for the cashier.

We came home with five tomato plants, and planted them in pots strategically lined up against the cottage wall to be protected from the wind while exposed to the sun and close to a source of water. In the last years of her life, my mother used to set her tomato plants against the neighbor's house blind wall, where they could soak up the heat collected by the cement after the sun had gone weaker. Not that we need such tricks in warm California, but Petaluma, where I live, can be windy, and following a family tradition felt good in these uncertain times.

We finally have thyme again, the culinary kind, which will spread at the feet of the gazebo, between climbing clematis and jasmine that hopefully will both wildly and obediently climb up and over the old painted iron structure, perhaps intermingling somewhere in the middle and creating odd combinations of colors and fragrances. We have Blue Lake green beans, three seedlings in a planter, three wooden stakes meeting at the top—teepee style—for the plants to sprawl up and cover territory in the air like a castle in a dream. We have Black Beauty zucchini. We have peas laid in two rows on either side of a hog fencing piece that will work as a ladder for them to hike the sky. We have a whole planter full of Swiss chard. All these starters seem to have survived the first few days of acclimation to new soil, new sun, and new orientation. Some of them are already thriving and have grown an extra inch, or leaf. I am hopeful, despite catching a sight of a spider first thing this morning—"araignée du matin, chagrin"—"spider in the morning, mourning," goes the saying in French.

Spiders, however, are terrific menders, so I remain hopeful against the silly French omen. Gardening has not been the only instrument of grace in this time of confinement and physical distancing. The animals—cats and dogs, sheep and goats, birds of all feathers, skunks and opossums, raccoons, shy deer and sly foxes—all have helped as well, tremendously, making us feel at home in our common territory. Now that we are not in such a rush as on regular work days, now that we take time to listen, and watch for subtle movement in the leaves, we catch sight of elusive visitors we didn't realize are regulars. We see more of our pets, greet and treat each other, at both ends of the day and many times in between. We know each other better, trust each other to be who we need, can, and want to be. We count on each other's presence, a furry neck pressing against my side, reaching into my hands, looking not for treat but for touch. We hold each other silently and enjoy together the brisk or gentle breath of wind on our cheeks.

You belong right here under the sun, I hear them say, still in the tenderness of April, although it's early May—not too hot, though soft enough to feel the warmth and not suffer from it. A lovely wind carries the rich aroma of earth still wet enough for recent rains to dress grass the color of Spring and give the lambs a sweetness to rival with their mother's milk. The sheep get drunk on it; giddy, they trust my hand full of grain. The rams do not protest in their usual jealous way to see the ewes welcome this offering of friendship, but sometimes bleat at a distance in awkward approval.

You, I hear them say, belong right here with your naked feet planted into sweet grass, and your bare legs shooting up ready to move you further, faster, wherever they can carry you. No chains in this nakedness of yours, no fear.

Every day you cross, whispers another voice inside my head, as you would a luscious field of grass, having done nothing of what your hand wrote yesterday on the list, or perhaps just one or two things, every one of these so-called lazy days tells you how much you need this pause, however forced by circumstances. So, you didn't paint today, or yesterday, or even the day before yesterday. And you still cherish that afternoon three days ago when the painting really talked to you, and you listened. You stepped away, and the satisfaction remained, because you enjoyed the full swell of it instead of rushing back into the feeling as if afraid that it would leave.

"But," I hear myself protest, "it might just leave and abandon me. Who is to tell that I was right to let it sit? Maybe I missed something."

And I, my sweet, the other voice insists, tell you didn't miss anything that you were not ready to see, take, pursue, or transform. You have to make the time to listen deeply, welcome the pause, feel the boredom and the restlessness, indulge in the lazing around reading books no one asked you to read, accommodate the need to rest between steps, so when you are ready, the next one will take you where you want to go, even if you don't know where that might be.

So, you didn't paint today, or yesterday, or whatever day followed that cherished afternoon when something got accomplished, but the feeling endured of accomplishment, and your hand got freer when it ventured at the portrait again. Messing with it, but with a measure of instinct and intent. Someone you don't quite know yet is holding the brush, deciding when to stop. You listened. Good for you! You did because you had removed yourself for a while from the task you had created for yourself—twenty-five 12x12 pieces by the end of May. You are almost there, right on schedule. Recreation is what you need now. Hope has returned after you tired of your vision and got discouraged. You rested, and now you see the end again, in all its modest and glorious proportions, a delight of its own no one else would have conceived that way.

Rest is good—what you call laziness—the rest your mother used to say you never knew to find. Restlessness your operating mode, because you knew what could be heard and felt in the stillness of rest threatened the voice urging you to find it.

~

I am looking forward to life after the pause, after the forced rest that taught me how to find my rhythm and be grateful for the clarity it is now weaving into my every move.

I learned of the vast expanses open to me when I slowed down and took the time to hear my fancy. What the next move will be will surprise me while falling into place as if by miracle. I am done rushing. Done running from duty to self-imposed tasks and expectations inherited from ancient lives. I will follow my whims at last, having taken the frivolous edge off and kept my eye on the root of desire, trusting its force and its wisdom, no longer chained in other people's expectations or my own will to serve and please. I have started to believe in my own good, my own star. I am on the right path, looking forward to carrying the pause inside of me, like a witch, pregnant with truths unsaid and beauty made of every walk of life, happy and sad, as a whole and round world should be.

Thursday the moon is full, and the new moon falls on the day I retire.

Plenty of time to face and feel desire. Plenty of time to act on it.

Prompt: What have you learned during the COVID-19 pandemic?

Monday, Covidian Time

Today, I swam,
and spent the rest of
the hours mostly
agonizing over
tangles of words,
trying to loosen
strands and weave a
single solid braid
easy to hold onto,
or pull.

Yesterday was all play,
a handful of words
arranged here
and not there—a few
paragraphs:
calm notice of
repetitions—
almost heard the call
to tighten and tidy
things around,
flip a page,
cut and paste,
give a random
piece an aim.
I saw the need and
did not act.

Sunday's for friends,
leisurely lunches,
massages and
bubbly rosé,
Sunday.

Monday spins the world
around, chickens
lay eggs again,
dogs lie in the way
—a chair, a window—
a woodpecker keeps
knocking at the siding,
flying off when I
open the door
only to wait and
to return after I fall
into the writing well,
forgetful of her persistent
desire
to peck a cavern in
our wall.

Saturday, I swam
and wished I were
a woodpecker
with a mission clearly
etched in the brain.
I know I will
let the bird
have her cut.

Friday, the news
pokes a hole
in my tender shell—
sad and grateful,
I sigh and wail.

I heard that Ruth
Bader Ginsburg was gone,
I heard she finally went out,
moved on,
but she did not step down,
my friend,
oh no, she didn't take
a bluesy step aside.

She pecked and drummed,
and tapped and jabbed
until we called
the color of
dissent.

Prompt: Write about your sense of time in confinement, during shelter in place.

What energizes you?

A swim early in the morning before breakfast, rain or shine, overcast preferred.

A dance jam with unexpected duets and discoveries, even if some are cause for grief and regrets.

The challenge of a new dance, a new project, an old friendship, a letter.

The surprise of a smiling face in the midst of doubt and sadness. A love boost. A request for help.

A new idea, a new friend, a task I know will bring relief, success to some perhaps. What is success? A different way of going about an old question.

The thought of a lovely creature I know, knew, or will soon meet.

A cat-nap.

A murmuration of starlings.

A morning walk in the mist.

Talks with the barnyard animals and other animals.

Epiphanies, big and small.

Christine Renaudin

Christine Renaudin lives, writes, and paints in Petaluma, CA. She is also a dancer and performs occasionally in the Bay Area—last seen on Halloween, haunting the entrance of the de Young Memorial Museum with a pride of witches. She likes to mix art forms, see what comes out, and share.

Her contributions to the first volume of Marlene Cullen's *The Write Spot* series, *Discoveries* include "Harvest," "If Only," "Ink," "Marie Pie Time," and "Thursday Rains."

Give Me Something

An instrument of time,
my kitchen clock doesn't know
the answer to a simple question.

What day is it?
Like talking to myself,
the only answer is silent hands,
slow unbending yoga, red face.

Time is slippery as
a street corner card sharp
wearing spiked hair
and a smoldering blazer.

Having heard angels are instruments of grace,
I grip one tightly—carved stone—an icon in my hand,
but angels are a complication to my philosophy.
I believe in them but do they believe in me?

About grace prevailing over time,
give me something I can grip:
hammer, pen, the lapels of a jacket,
and I promise to believe what you say.

Prompt: During shelter in place, have you discovered what works for you as an "instrument of grace?"

Fox Trot

A curtain parted, beaded, of mustard grass.
Fox made an entrance and trotted across
an asphalt stage, expanse of empty parking spaces
stained with motor oil. Without missing a step.
The audience was wind, full of bluster,
phrased with pollen mitigated by a whisper
of unseen lilac. But the fox was seen
despite having gotten scent, or sixth sense,
college was closed, cars and people absent.
The fox's coat was the color of caramelized sugar.
He/she/they paused like a debutante waiting
to be conferred royal title, the applause of a suitor,
but it was my nose that was in the air.
My heart on my sleeve hid a heart tattoo.
What is happiness, I asked, what sweetness
has been missing? But the fox didn't answer.
Did the fox want to be seen frozen,
skilled as lawn statuary unmoved by wind?
Or did the fox just not want to give audience
dancing in a coat the color of caramelized sugar?

Prompt: Waiting.

Portrait of Self as Hero

On what concrete, mahogany, or other choice pedestals
do you coronate your heroes after standing awe-struck,
shaking, unable to shake their hands? Do you simply
throw down your signed photographs of sluggers and starlets
upon a pile of relics when you return home,
the curtains looking drab? Or sometimes do you feel like
your own hero, mornings, only to watch storm clouds build,
the kind that appear in cartoons, purple, threatening,
thunderous as Father figures? Their words of negation—
at times all it took was the tone of their voices—to make you
want to disappear into a place six feet under, into the womb
of the earth. Words—are they what's the matter—forget
 them
and compare your self-portrait to the faces of your heroes—
see—eyes—nose—lips—what else do you need to sense
the strength rising within as you grow beyond
 comprehension,
like a tree into this earth standing on your own two feet?

Prompt: Write a persona poem. Also known as a dramatic monologue, this form shares many characteristics with a theatrical monologue: an audience is implied; there is no dialogue; and the poet writes in a voice other than his or her own, adopting the voice of a fictional character, which could be someone ordinary or someone famous. Definition adapted from: www.poets.org/glossary/persona-poem.

What energizes you?

What energizes me is nature, specifically her unexpected gifts. I say gifts because, along with my mother and father, nature has already given me life. Nature provides the home I live in. Trees provide the wood frame. Calcium carbonate (also known as lime), cement, and sand, make up the stucco exterior walls. When melted and cooled, sand even provides the raw material for the windows through which I stare out at nature. Nature also provides the air I breathe, the food I eat, and the water I drink, in other words, all I really need. Anything extra is a gift.

On a nature walk, when an unexpected flock crosses my path, and the flash of color tells me they are goldfinches, my heart flutters as if pulsing with confetti instead of blood. My skin sprouts pins and needles as if pierced by dozens of Siberian squill, those tiny, rare, late winter bulbs that push living purple into the coldest snowbank. Days like that, I'm filled with joy for hours, and find myself going about the most mundane chores of living happily, in brotherhood with the goldfinch, my own heart, and even the deepest snowfall.

Dave Seter

Dave Seter is the author of *Don't Sing to Me of Electric Fences*, a poetry collection due out from Cherry Grove Collections in 2021. A civil engineer and poet, he writes about social and environmental issues, including the intersection of the built world and the natural world. Born in Chicago, he now lives in Sonoma County, California. He earned his undergraduate degree in civil engineering from Princeton University and his graduate degree in humanities from Dominican University of California, where he studied ecopoetics.

Boss Lady and the Monkey

Sometimes there's magnificent grace and beauty in what's *not* there. Just ask any cancer patient who's been praying for a clean MRI. Ask the parent who feels all of the gripping in her stomach release when her child safely returns home after a first solo journey with the car keys. Our loved ones call and act as if everything is A-OK just when we've spiraled into a deep fear fest, and we exhale to release and empty all the invisible torment. When all of our doom scrolling, every catastrophic scenario we can conjure up, and all the imagined monsters under the bed turn out to be non-existent, we can be extraordinarily grateful for the absences of things.

This idea can work in other ways, too. You know that moment when you wake up before dawn, and the house is quiet? Maybe you tune into the hum of the furnace or that sound of the flame igniting as you light the stove and prepare to heat the kettle for the morning tea. In the midst of it all, before it all, there's an absence of something that seems to have an ancient resonance. It's silent and still there in the twilight for just a moment. No birdsongs yet. And before your children are happily chirping. There's a threshold between silence and sound where both nothing exists and everything exists. And we can live there for just a moment.

Meditation practitioners speak of that slice of eternity between the inhale and the exhale. That elusive moment when we can turn off all of our longing, rumination, interior soundtracks, and be empty of it all. Maybe it lasts a second or two. But it's there. Buddhist teachers of the Dharma tell us that all we need to do to stretch that moment out is still our monkey mind, the part of our thinking that is restless and unsettled. The part that insists on exploring dinner options and movie plots in the middle of a downward-facing dog.

In the past, I spent so much of my life grasping, strategizing and controlling, that being still and quiet seemed like staring up at Mt. Everest from basecamp. My monkey mind merged with my ego and became an overachiever on meth. She giddily escorted me to every worst-case scenario as if we were two BFFs heading off on a Vegas weekend bender. She held my hand and showed me how bad it could get if I didn't remain vigilant. She considered it her absolute mission to remind me I had signed that *3P Contract* to Perfect, Please, and Prove. And, most annoyingly, she'd also kept a running tally of what I hadn't accomplished and stood there with a checklist and pencil. She was persistent and loud, not only during my half-hearted attempts to meditate but all through the day.

Many scenarios brought her noise level up to decibels that rivaled a thrash metal concert. There was the mandated mantra to be a good mother (whatever that means). The rule books said to be an overachiever at work by never putting in an hour on a project when three and a half will do. I had to be the smartest person in the room to push back feelings of vulnerability and echoes of inadequacy. During conversations with both casual acquaintances and people I professed to love, I was only half present while thinking of what I would say next or replaying what I had just said to see how it had landed. Of course, I had to do it all with the right brand of concealer and a pair of wicked boss-lady, badass shoes.

That was my life for a very long time. In all of those scenarios, what *wasn't* there was authenticity, honoring relationships, silence, and the poise and elegance that arrives through grace. It was, of course, always there waiting for me. I just had to get the monkey to release the gear shift and the gas pedal. It wasn't as easy as the Buddhist monks made it sound.

But I eventually learned when I got serious about being quiet and listening, the matching grant from the universe that I'd always heard about became real. Every spiritual tradition urges prayer, contemplation, and some practice of exploring the rich interior life we all share. I always thought it was a monologue. The transformative moment for me was when I realized it's a *dialogue*. Sometimes it sounds like a whisper that only lives in my head. Sometimes it's a line from a poem or an off-handed remark from a stranger. It's a call and response kind of communication that requires a subtle (or not so subtle) shifting of thought or action. For the past few years, it's been my steady companion:

Follow your heart, it urged, as it showed me how to take those heels and walk out on a 30-year career.

Have compassion, it murmured, as it navigated me through the suicidal struggles and deaths of loved ones.

Forgive yourself and others, it patiently pleaded, as it guided me through every dark cave of chemo treatments.

And somehow, all of that makes perfect, beautiful, messy sense. When I learned to trust it, I was finally ready to take that monkey's hand and gently walk her back to the safety of her soft, green shelter.

The Irish say that it's the holes in their lacework that make the pieces beautiful. It's the empty spaces that define what's there. The same could be said about the Japanese art of bonsai. The balance is in the potent negative areas that surround the branches and the foliage. Ultimately, the voids, the silences, the blank spaces are not the absence of something—rather, they are the presence of something. What's not there, when we take the time to be still, is our greatest gift. And each time my little monkey friend returns, as she's prone to do, I can be grateful because she's a powerful reminder for me to become silent and honor the mystery of that eternal whisper.

Prompt: Write about a time when a perceived loss turned into a win.

Lullabies and Anthems

Both physicists and singer-songwriter Joni Mitchell tell us that we're all bits of stardust. We're made up of atoms that come from stars that exploded long ago—frozen light connected to the grand, swirling cosmos with our every inhale and exhale. It's hard to fathom that as we do the grocery shopping or pick up the dry cleaning. Every mundane, precarious, and tragically lived experience can take us further and further from the truth. But sometimes, like when we behold the sublime purity of a newborn baby or serendipitously stumble upon a Mozart aria floating through a stranger's open window, we find ourselves staring the glorious truth straight in the eye. In such moments, we remember our own purity and beauty and acknowledge a primordial echo that says. *Yes, this is you too, my love.*

That newborn baby girl is an invitation to remember our own journey to this earthly plane. Just like her, we arrived in wide-eyed wonder—open and free with the residue of stardust in our eyes. Like our ancient ancestors, we emerged from the liquid velvet of the womb into the earth's cool air in order to remember. Remember our sacred mission. Remember our holy lineage. Remember that we are *life* itself, connected to every blossom and bud, connected to the force of the river's current and the ocean's roar. We are specks of stardust and solar systems all at once. Never separate from love, never alone.

That unexpected aria that soars through the breeze and lands directly in our heart when we least expect it reminds us of the power of grace. It stops us in our tracks and invites us to acknowledge the blessings that are so easily missed. We trip over everyday miracles as we rush to the post office. Somehow we lose sight of the unalterable truth. We lose our way through the galaxy in the midst of being human. We feel alone in the darkness and begin to ponder what we once knew with certainty.

Twinkle, twinkle, little star, how I wonder what you are.

At such times, we need comfort and the assurance of a lullaby. But instead, in response to all of life's hard human lessons and injuries, we grow armor year after year. As our armor strengthens, it dims our sweet starlight. We learn to hide our radiance so that no one can take it from us. We keep our flame secret so that it won't go out like a fickle pilot light. Little by little, we begin to forget our own brilliance and our ability to shine. We stop dancing with the universe and forget how to laugh with our life-force. However, thankfully, our light is constant, even when dim. Its flicker is an ever-present sacrament, and we can find it—even in the darkest of times.

Like a diamond in the sky.

We can remember what the world forgot. We can affirm that we are a part of a much larger, magnificent whole. A star, within a constellation, within a galaxy, within a universe, within the cosmos. We are marvelously interconnected, a part of both the psalms and the sands of time. And, when we remember that, we can offer it up to others. We can love bravely and open-heartedly, and we can fully forgive every earthly slight and misstep—especially our own. Then, our soft light becomes a bright beacon. Our little lullaby becomes a bold anthem proclaiming that we are, and always have been, as Joni Mitchell says, golden.

Prompt: "The stars we are given. The constellations we make. That is to say, stars exist in the cosmos, but constellations are the imaginary lines we draw between them, the readings we give the sky, the stories we tell."—Rebecca Solnit

What I Won't Tell You

I've never practiced an acceptance speech for that moment when I triumphantly extend my arm high into the air to pump an Academy Award Oscar statuette up toward the heavens. And, truthfully, I've never risen early on an October morning and expected to take a call from the Nobel Committee in Stockholm—just so you know, because of the time zone difference, the call would probably come in the middle of the night. Sure, maybe once or twice I've fantasized about how humble and self-deprecating I'd be while discussing my MacArthur Genius Grant or how articulate and insightful I'd come off when being interviewed by Terry Gross. When Terry or some other deftly literate NPR journalist asks about the newly released story of my life, I'll have my response all queued up. After graciously thanking them for the opportunity, I'll begin by stating, "My story is about all of the things I *won't* tell you."

"It's not really about being an adopted child who found herself in a home with unhappy parents, for example. I'm not going to tell you about that. It's more about finding beautiful, imperfect, wobbly replacements for everything I didn't have. For instance, I can tell you what my grandparents' love looked like in great detail. There's the way my grandfather popped popcorn on the stove, old-school style. He'd heat the oil in a dented saucepan, wait for it to sizzle, pour the kernels in, and then pretend he couldn't find the lid—every single time. My brother and I would race around the kitchen, trying to find something with which to cover the pot while popcorn shot in all directions and hot kernels ricocheted off the cabinets. My grandfather played it stone-cold deadpan and would look around the room and calmly say, 'Now, where did your grandmother put that lid?' As my brother and I happily picked up every errant piece of popped goodness, we'd act like exasperated school teachers and say, 'Grandpa, you're supposed to have the lid ready *before* you begin.' This scene played out dozens of times, and each of us had our cherished roles and lines memorized.

"Before our weekly visits, Grandpa hid coins in pill bottles beneath the floorboards of his attic. My parents would drop us off, and he'd greet us at the front door. Without saying hello, we'd run past him and race up the stairs, eager to find our treasure. There was joy in that house. We arrived hungry to shake off the heaviness of a depressed mother and an angry father while our British grandmother, in a house dress and heels, put TV dinners and frozen pizzas into the oven—not because she didn't want to cook from scratch for us but, rather, because that's what we asked her to make.

"My story is not really about feeling like an odds-against-her outsider from the very beginning. It's more about the drawings I drew and the stories I dreamed up in an effort to save myself. Before I was old enough to leave the house for solo journeys on my bike, I could use my imagination to transport myself far from my working-class, Northwest-side Chicago neighborhood. I not only had an imaginary friend—I invented a whole damn fictional family. I made the characters, scenes, dialogue, and plot lines in my head correspond to everything I didn't see in my world. My imaginary family was happy. We lived an idyllic, tree-house, hippy sort of life in the forests of the Pacific Northwest. In my third-grade theater of the mind fantasy, things we needed just magically appeared while we lived like woodland sprites playing pan flutes. As a kid, I could draw a whole flow chart of this imaginary world for you.

"A few years later, instead of a bike, I took a dirty, exhaust-belching bus away from my frame house every Wednesday afternoon and traveled toward glittering skyscrapers, the lakefront, and dozens of museums in a journey that may as well have been a moon landing. I sat in the dark basement of a lecture hall in the Art Institute of Chicago, waking up for the first time while taking an AP Art History class. I felt sparks dance in my heart, and I swear I heard pan flute music as I saw the ways humans create art to make sense of their world. I viewed slides of Etruscan vases, Egyptian artifacts, and fragments of the Sistine Chapel. Fertility goddesses and Andy Warhol's soup cans were equally mystifying invitations toward a stance of wonder. In that basement, I found a set of wings. As my teenage world opened up, I gratefully realized that in addition to complaining about the price of a gallon of milk, people could choose to talk about grand ideas."

We can debate about abstract concepts like truth and beauty and speak passionately about love in magnificently meager attempts to describe what's ineffable.

Maybe there'll be a pause in the interview for the pledge drive promo or a moment for a sip of water. Then, I'll continue. "My story isn't really about a relationship with a sweetheart who actually wasn't very sweet or fully capable of feeling what was in his heart. I won't tell you that the two of us were so wounded that we clung to each other out of desperation rather than self-actualization. It's more about the little soul who joined us—the child who gave me the final push to imagine something better and, eventually, the courage to leave. Her name, Grace, is a cosmic wink.

"I won't tell you about being a divorced, single mother and all of the tropes, stereotypes, and disasters that people like to imagine. You already know about those. Instead, I'll talk about adventures with Grace. I'll recount memories of holding her tiny hands and swinging her in circles while laughing hard and becoming so dizzy that we both collapsed onto Lake Michigan sand, staring up into skies that extended into the stratosphere. I'll tell you that we traveled as a tag-team duo. And that we walked through airports and city streets with a sense of curiosity and wonder. She carried a tiny wheeled suitcase that held her pajamas and all of her future aspirations to change the world.

"Finally, I won't spend any time recounting the many struggles that Grace has had growing up in a world where girls often internalize hurtful, conflicting messages about their bodies and dreams as consistently as they take in oxygen. I won't tell you about my breast cancer journey. What I will say to you is that the path I've traveled has put me in the perfect classroom, at the perfect time, every time. That statement about classrooms is both literal and metaphorical. In fact, the moments when I felt the most joy and fulfillment in a thirty-year career as an educator occurred when I saw myself as a student rather than a teacher. I'll let you know that ten years ago, I finally found a real sweetheart, a man who is kind and knows his way around the landscape of his own heart and mine. We travel all over the world—you know, when there's not a global pandemic. We make great meals together, and we've made a family that honors love and finds courage in the willingness to be vulnerable. Even when it's really messy. My running joke these days, as the COVID-19 lockdown restrictions continue, is that it feels as though we went underwater in a submarine back at the start of the pandemic and haven't emerged yet. But, ultimately, I suppose my story is about many moments of re-emerging, rerouting, and reimagining."

At this point, I suspect Terry Gross might be ready to wrap up our segment. After all, she's got politicians, celebrities, and real luminaries to interview. As I make a final few pithy and profound comments, I'll consider offering a spoiler alert so as not to ruin the story's ending for the audience. Then, I'll decide against it and let everyone know that there's a happy ending. Because, sometimes, the kindest way for a storyteller to properly acknowledge pain, grief, and loss involves helping others to imagine what a set of wings might look like.

Prompt: Pretend you have written a book—the story of your life. Imagine you are being interviewed about your story.

What energizes you?

A few predictable energy boosters are on my daily must-have list: A nice pot of perfectly-brewed jasmine green tea, for instance. There's yoga and a spiritual practice that gets the life-force moving in just the right direction without fail. Music, listened to at decibels that are probably a bit dangerous and, frankly, a little embarrassing for a woman of a certain age, always does the trick. Writing something true, even if it's fiction, is better than a caffeine high. Conversations that are the opposite of small-talk—the ones that are equal parts honest, brilliant, touching, and a bit spicy light me up like fireworks.

Then, I go outside, and there's the turbo charge, rocket-booster type of energy that comes from the natural world. I find it on a Midwestern springtime walk when the redbud blossoms are vibrating electric-neon pink. It's there again as the bulbs we planted in the fall burst into a tulip riot right there in the front yard. There's seeing my breath turn into ice crystals like mid-air magic in February. Did I mention autumn? There's stargazing and big, bold bodies of water that hold the secrets of the universe. Every time I think I've seen nature's best show, I'm proven wrong. And that energizes me more than anything.

Deb Fenwick

Deb Fenwick is a Chicago-born writer who currently lives in Oak Park, Illinois. After spending nearly thirty years working as an arts educator, school program specialist, youth advocate, and public school administrator, she now considers herself a full-time beauty hunter. When she's not traveling with her heartthrob of a husband or dreaming up wildly impractical adventures with her intrepid, college-age daughter, you'll find her out in the garden getting muddy with two little pups.

Julie Wilder-Sherman

A Blackboard and a Black Rose

1963. November. Anticipation of Thanksgiving.

Coming soon! Smells of turkey, cinnamon, and pumpkin pie. The Macy's parade on our black and white TV. Cousins. Dressing up. The grown-up table set with the special china, the good silver, the gravy boat. The kids' table for me and my cousins, complete with tablecloth, linen napkins, glassware, and a paper honeycomb turkey in the middle. Special treats in the fancy glass bowls with scalloped edges filled with chocolate truffles and cream cheese-filled dates. The anticipation of this family holiday makes me fidgety and chatty.

School. Fifth grade. Band room. Mrs. King with her blueish silver hair, eyeglasses hanging on a chain around her neck, walks swiftly into the practice room and whispers in Mr. Salinger's ear. He tells us to put our instruments away and return to our classes quietly and quickly. I disassemble my silver flute and place it carefully in the maroon-colored velvet padded case. We obediently walk back to our classrooms.

Our teacher, Miss Phelps, usually smiling and welcoming, looks different. She is not smiling. I notice that her mouth is set, her jaw looks tight, and her skin is whiter than usual. She tells us to sit down quietly. She passes out the good paper, the white smooth paper that is saved for special work, not the pale tan newsprint we use for practicing sentence diagrams and listing verbs.

She tells us to copy what she writes on the blackboard. She writes the date, November 22, 1963, and the words, "A shot has been fired and the world is in stillness. President

John F. Kennedy has been assassinated in Dallas, Texas." I learn a new word that day.

She puts the chalk down, turns slowly from the blackboard and faces the class. Her hands clasped together at her waist, she speaks quietly and tells us to sign our names—and to keep the piece of paper forever as it will be part of history. I understand that something big and horrible has happened, but I do not understand the weightiness of the tragedy, or what it means to be a part of history. I realize that this is not a time to shift in my seat or whisper to a friend.

We are dismissed early and told to go straight home. My parents work, so I expect the house to be empty when I climb the twelve speckled marble steps and unlock the front door to our gray San Francisco flat. I am surprised to see my mother is home. She is crying. The television is on, which is strange because the television is never on during the day. My father comes home. His eyes are red rimmed.

My mother hangs a black velvet rose on our front door. We eat dinner in front of the TV. There is no taste. Black and gray images flicker on the screen, people crying, Walter Cronkite with his calm yet slightly shaky voice keeps the American people informed. His coat is off.

The mood in the house is still and heavy. My father openly cries, his head hanging down, hands clasped together as though in prayer. His shoulders jerk up and down slightly. It is the first time I see my father cry. It is unsettling to me.

The black rose is stolen from our front door. Thanksgiving is different that year.

Prompt: Poem: Our House to Your House by Joseph Ridl.

Yesterday's Goodbye, Today's Hello

Yesterday was tears and sobs,
hunched shoulders over a soft limp body with fixed eyes.
Calling his name. Calling his name
in disbelief,
willing him to come back.
Yesterday my heart shattered over and over with each gulp
and gasp.
Yesterday was endless.

Yesterday was an empty dog bed, a house quiet and still,
his absence felt in every room.
Yesterday was donated toys to the animal shelter
and giving his dog treats to neighbors.
Yesterday was photographs and condolence cards in the
mailbox
sprinkled with spilled tears, then displayed on the piano.
Yesterday he walked the rainbow bridge.
Yesterday was Mushu's goodbye.

Yesterday was a dawning.
Yesterday was a lesson learned.
Yesterday was a decision
to glue together the pieces of my shattered heart and to
love again.
Yesterday was surrender to what I knew was waiting for me
allowing me to say goodbye and whisper hello.

Today is fresh smells and sniffs outside.
Today is squeals and laughter and piddles on the floor.
Today is a cocked head, a robust fast-wagging tail, a playful nip at my ankle, and chasing a slipper down the hall.
Today is new toys, a new bowl, and the smell of puppy breath.
Today is fresh eyes and hope for years ahead
with days at the beach, walks on trails, and a sleepy sigh next to me on the couch
at the end of the day.
Today is a heart still mending, yet open and hoping for countless adventures and many years.
Today is new love, fresh air, and a deep breath.
Today is Juno's hello.

Prompt: A realization or epiphany about a loss.

An Ordinary Day

Waves will surge and subside, rolling up into white foamy bubbles reaching my toes. I'll sink slightly into the beach's soft warm sand. A breeze will blow gently and steadily, fanning my hair in different directions.

After an hour of walking, my husband and I will go into town and find a cafe teeming with people. We'll hear them laughing and clinking glasses, join them at a table community style, blend into their conversations and make one-day friends.

We'll sit close, exchanging knowing looks of having survived, acknowledging what it took to get back to appreciating the ordinary without having to say so. We'll see each fully exposed face, open and smiling, not a mask in sight.

We'll chat and chuckle while enjoying cold beers and flame-broiled burgers with fries. There won't be a disinfectant bottle on the table or near the door. We will feel so comfortable talking with the table of strangers that, as we leave, I'll go over to the mother-to-be with her basketball belly and give her a gentle hug. "Good luck with your baby," I'll whisper in her ear and she'll respond with a radiant smile, touching my hand as I leave. The purity of receiving a simple stroke of another's hand will feel familiar and natural.

My husband and I will get into our car without spraying our palms with sanitizer. We'll drive to visit friends and embrace them in long bear hugs, rock back and forth in the grip, exclaim how much we've missed them, look into their smiling faces, then hug again.

Our daughters will show up at the front door and we will hold them with a feeling of never letting go. We'll kiss their faces, our fingers in their hair, then nuzzle and sniff them the way a new mama dog nuzzles and sniffs her newborn puppies.

Our neighbors will gather outside on our narrow street, and instead of calling from opposite sides of the sidewalks, we will move near each other when we chat, speaking at a normal conversational volume. Six feet apart will become three feet apart, then two. We'll clasp hands, pat each other on the backs, and embrace like we've been away at war, never again taking for granted a simple, ordinary day.

Prompt: What are you looking forward to when shelter in place is over?

What energizes you?

"Honey, what energizes me?" I asked my husband.

Without a moment's hesitation, he said, "Projects."

"Projects?" I replied. "What do you mean?"

"When you decide to sink your teeth into something, when you set your mind to a task and you get it done, you're energized."

"Oh," I mused. "I never realized that."

So, I started thinking, and it occurred to me that he was right. When I started a video project for my twin daughters, I was completely focused, refusing to let anything distract me or pull me away. While working on that project, I realized I was really, really happy and excited. And yes, I was energized.

When I began working on my mother's surprise birthday party, for two months I could think of or talk about nothing else—from the decorations and music, to the table setup and birthday signs, right down to the cupcake toppers. And I realize now, looking back, that while working on that party, I was joyful, and jubilant.

When I decided to become a gardener and beautify the small space to the side of my house, I was all in. With dirt up to my elbows and the smell of fresh soil surrounding me, I literally and figuratively dug in, invigorated by Earth's gifts.

When asked to participate in a local political movement whose ideologies matched mine, I joined with verve and determination, feeling uplifted and motivated by the possibility of helping our nation return to the path of fairness, honor, and decency.

I am galvanized by the thought of something new, the challenge and expectation that the project, the venture, the unknown waiting to be known will reveal itself to be beautiful, delightful, stunning, perhaps splendid.

I am energized by the simple things in life like hosting a birthday party, working in dirt, fighting for democracy, and seeing the joy on others' faces hopefully mirroring my own.

Julie Wilder-Sherman

San Francisco native Julie Wilder-Sherman is a long-time resident of Petaluma, California. She began reading books at an early age, encouraged by her mother, who would allow her to take books to bed when she was as young as two years old. Julie would "read" until she was ready to go to sleep. To this day, Julie reads every night before turning out the lights.

Raised in a family of readers, writers, performers, musicians, and political activists, Julie followed her dream of singing professionally. While working on *The Love Boat* as a featured singer for Princess Cruises, she met her husband, bassist Jeff Sherman. Together they have traveled the world.

After leaving the cruise business, Julie worked for The Branson School for eight years before moving on to Autodesk where she was the Community Relations Manager for worldwide charitable giving for 18 years.

After retiring in 2018, Julie became politically active, and she continues to help manage the Petaluma Postcard Pod, an organization that supports Democratic principles and ideals.

With retirement offering her the gift of time, Julie has explored new areas of interest: writing, cooking, and gardening. The mother of twin girls, opera singer Camille Sherman and music production assistant Emily Sherman, Julie resides in a little house with her husband, two cats, and a dog while enjoying writing, eating well and reading in her garden.

A Perfect Moment

The air hung heavy. The sun ignited the dust, giving it heft and dimension; illuminating specks as they floated and shimmered. I drew in a breath, flavored by the pungent, oaky soil, and let the warmth settle in my chest. It was late August in California. My husband and I were spending the weekend with his parents at their cozy, A-frame home, nestled in the foothills below Placerville.

I adored it here in the summertime, especially when the creek still held water. Everything moved at a slower pace; country roads and simple life. As I walked along the empty backroad, bucket in hand, I glanced sideways at Bonnie, my mother-in-law. God, I loved Bonnie. Short and solid, she exuded such radiance and joie de vivre that she was a summer day unto herself. Bawdy laugh, razor wit, Bonnie was always curious, and eager to drink a person in. She crackled with life. There was never enough time in the day to spend with her; we could talk from dawn to dusk and still have so much to say. Being with Bonnie was easy, like slipping into a favorite pair of worn jeans.

As we chatted our way up the quiet lane, trickles of sweat ran down my back, and I reveled in the way the sun kissed my skin. "Just up here is my favorite spot," Bonnie pointed, "the berries always seem to be better." I could feel my mouth begin to water. Bonnie was right, these were some of the plumpest blackberries I had ever seen. The bushes were alive with fruit.

"I'm just having one," I promised, "the rest will go in the pail." Bonnie turned her brown, laughing eyes on me. "Yeah, right," she chuckled.

I plucked a giant berry, nimbly avoiding the brambles surrounding it. I popped it into my mouth, closed my eyes, and was swept away. The blackberry, toasted by the afternoon sun, was lush and ripe. It exploded in a swirl of flavor, coating my throat like thick syrup. As I groaned, Bonnie laughed her exuberant laugh. We both knew we'd be lucky to make it home with even one full bucket.

Underneath a bower of swaying oak trees, creek burbling below, picking berries with my beloved friend, I allowed myself one of those prayer moments. An overwhelming rush of gratitude flowed through me.

I looked at Bonnie, who was nibbling at a blackberry. We grinned at each other, and her eyes twinkled.

On this summer afternoon, we had shared a perfect moment.

Prompt: A favorite summertime memory.

Anxiety

Hello darkness, my old friend. We've got to stop meeting like this, in the middle of the night, so intimate, so intense. My husband sleeps next to me.

Peaceful.

Clueless.

Shhhh.

You wrap yourself around me seductively, cloying and familiar. You are my bad habit, the one I try to bury and keep hidden. Your tendrils follow familiar paths through my mind, wafting down the narrow hallways, scraping fingernails along the plaster. You leave scars upon scars.

We dance. This too has become routine. We have perfected the steps. We tango like old lovers, the darkness and the light. Your grip on me is iron, your domination complete. I reel under your power.

You throb in my blood, running free in the silence of shadows that overwhelm me. Anxiety powered by vulnerability, fueled by fear—my oldest, primal self—slick and unbearably intrusive. You are my eternal companion when the sun sets. My brain spins and I give in to you.

Finally, we embrace, and I allow myself to be swallowed whole. Consumed. Together we watch the clock tick the hours down. The middle of the night belongs to us. I hate you, but I know no life without you. As the sun comes up, you skulk away.

You will return.

You always do.

Prompt: In the middle of the night.

Karen Handyside Ely

Surviving Shelter in Place

2020 has been the longest year of my life, and it's only April. I really can't complain (although that has never stopped me before). My adult children, who live in New York City, are healthy and still employed. My husband and I are well, and since I started hoarding toilet paper back in the '80s (that is an OCD story for another day) we are literally "good to go."

I've noticed as the days drag by, that I'm slowly getting used to this new reality. Getting used to it, and getting fat. In the very beginning, back in "aught March," I decided that this was an opportunity to actively pursue FINALLY becoming skinny. I've now failed four diets in four weeks. It doesn't help to have a husband who loves to bake. In the best of times, his sourdough is hard to resist. In these worst of times, I have given up trying. By the time I am able to physically spend time with friends in the flesh, I will have become a sphere.

For now, I've had to content myself with Zoom meet-ups. I am no spring chicken, and admit that I had never even heard of this video-conferencing platform. Hilarity ensued as I tried to be an old dog learning a new trick, a humbling yet rewarding experience. I'm now able to attend meetings, writing groups, and Happy Hours with friends from all over the globe. This too is a double-edged sword; the vino flows much more freely when you are sitting in your own kitchen, watching a screen, and missing your buds—another contributing factor to my expanding girth.

My writing has taken on a rather feast or famine existence. When writing on my own, the words either pour out on the page like torrential rain, or they dribble and drab like a leaky faucet; NO in between. Every Tuesday, I "Zoom" with a small gathering of friends, and we freewrite together. There is something so intimate about this virtual experience, and no, it is not because pants aren't required to attend. This new reality has become a sort of bonding mechanism between us, which enhances the writing sessions. I write with a sharper focus during these group endeavors, even as my self-disciple has gone the way of my diets. I had hoped to have cranked out a book by now, so much free time and all, but while I have fallen woefully short on quantity, I am progressing with quality.

I've been spending an abundance of time in my music room, which is filled with instruments that were played by my daughter, my son, and me over many years. I'm very rusty, and the piano needs tuning, but when I close my eyes, I am able to remember some of the songs that we collaborated on. Sadly, my fingers don't recollect quite as well, but the music brings me solace, even with the clinkers.

I've read several good books, along with some trashy romance novels. I've watched some stellar movies, and binged on some Netflix series that I am embarrassed to admit I watched. Sometimes a little junk is good for the soul, but I dream of the day that the Santa Rosa Symphony returns to the Green Center, and I can go back to gorging on beautiful, live music. I have also put myself on a strict news diet—only one hour of televised news a day. It is the one diet that I have not yet failed, and I am feeling much more fit, at least mentally.

To relieve stress, I stand in my backyard and howl every evening at 8 pm. No, I haven't lost it. Howling has become quite a thing here in Petaluma. It feels so good to let-er-rip, not a scream, but a loud, long, mournful howl. Even more gratifying than making this primal sound, is hearing neighbors howl back. It reminds me that we are in this together, and promises that we will get through this as a community.

Togetherness has taken on a completely different meaning since the onset of this quarantine. My husband and I do almost everything together. We take long walks, discovering nooks and crannies in this town that we've always been too busy to explore; albeit with covered faces. We twist ourselves into ridiculous pretzels every afternoon, as we try to maintain some semblance of a yoga practice. We spend so much time together, that a fifteen-minute shower alone feels like a solo week-end getaway. I don't know how he does it ... puts up with so much "us time"... right now I am even sick of myself.

I am tremendously blessed in many ways. I have slowed down, and learned to savor the small, everyday things in life. I revel in the bees buzzing among our wildflowers, soak up the sunset behind my oak tree, and taste the love that my wonderful husband pours into every meal that he makes—although I'm hoping he'll love me with salad a little more often. With kindness, compassion, and a strong dose of humor, this too shall pass.

Prompt: How has your life changed with shelter in place?

What energizes you?

If you had asked me this question last year, I would have reeled off a list of my favorite things: travel, being in nature, running. Between shelter in place, local fires, and personal health issues, I've had to reconfigure the activities that energize me. My imagination has been my biggest booster in these trying times. It has helped me to create spaces where I restore my vitality.

I bought a little blow-up pool, and my imagination did the rest. I travelled to Hawaii, Scottsdale, Miami, Cabo, and the Bahamas, from the comfort of my own backyard, complete with silk flower leis, colorful cacti, inflatable flamingos, and regional music. My fabulous husband James took his role as "cabana boy" very seriously, serving cold cerveza and fruity tropical drinks poolside.

I ran, virtually, across Great Britain and around the Ring of Kerry using my home elliptical machine and an app called The Conqueror. I explored quintessential English hamlets, verdant countryside, and Roman ruins, all on my computer screen. I imagined inhaling the crisp Irish mist, while smoke from the Northern California fires obliterated the view out my window.

James and I picnicked in a Moroccan medina on our living room floor. With exotic food, lots of pillows, and a smidge of imagination we were transported halfway around the world. We fed each other hummus and baba ganoush while reminiscing about past travels, and planning new adventures.

In 2020, my imagination has been what reinvigorates me, providing energy, motivation, and joy.

Karen Handyside Ely

There are some who swear that Karen Handyside Ely was born with her nose firmly planted in a book. She is a lifelong, voracious reader with an insatiable appetite for unusual words, lilting phrases, and absurd stories. After a brief stint as a credit analyst in San Francisco and New York City, and a 30-year career as a mom and "professional" volunteer in Scottsdale, AZ, Karen returned to her beloved hometown of Petaluma, CA.

She delights in difficult crossword puzzles, the Santa Rosa Symphony, and anything baked by her husband James.

Karen has been published in *The Write Spot to Jumpstart Your Writing: Discoveries*, *The Write Spot: Reflections*, *The Write Spot: Possibilities*, and *The Write Spot: Writing as a Path to Healing* (all available on Amazon).

First Kiss

The band was loud and off key. And then he kissed me.
The gym was packed with dancing teens. And then he kissed me.
The chaperones stood in a line at the back of the gym. And then he kissed me.
My heartbeat echoed the beat of the drum. And then he kissed me.
His hands were sweaty. So were mine. And then he kissed me.
I don't remember the name of the song. And then he kissed me.
He leaned in. I stood on tiptoes. And then he kissed me.
Chaperones surged. We were pulled apart. But he had kissed me.
The music stopped. But he had kissed me.
Parents were called. But he had kissed me.
I was grounded for a week. But he had kissed me.
Freedom at last. He came to my house. We went for a walk. And then he kissed me.
The rest is history.

Prompt: Write about a first-time experience.

I Can

I reported to work early
My work boots scuffed but clean
My jeans patched
My cap, though frayed and faded, shaded my eyes

The foreman called us over
"No more work," he said
"There's no demand"
How do I tell my wife I have no job

We have two growing boys to feed
And an acre of ground with a garden
A milk cow and some chickens
We will get by

I can plow the field
Plant the seeds
Milk the cow
Hoe the weeds

I served my country in the Great War
The war to end all wars
It wasn't
But it nearly ended me

Now I serve my family
I don't have my health

I can't do what I did
I can do what I can

I can repair the roof
Fix the truck
Clean the barn
Paint the house

I don't have a job
I can't do what I did
I can do what I can
We will get by

Prompt: What are you noticing?

I wrote this on Day 43 of shelter in place. I thought of my grandfather who served in WWI and was injured, then lived through the Spanish Flu and the Great Depression.

A Perfect Day

I swing gently back and forth on the porch swing, drinking in every sight, sound, and scent:

The sharp tang of the resin from the porch roof releasing its oils as it bakes in the sun

The soft shine of the painted floor reflecting the light

The dappled shade on the lawn from the ancient spreading oak tree

The whisper of air that caresses my face as I swing back and forth

The songs the birds sing from the branches of the trees

The sound of my children laughing as they chase a ball across the lawn

The green scent of grass being mown next door

The drone of the lawnmower

The clink of ice and the refreshing, cool taste of lemonade with its perfect balance of tart and sweet

The heady perfume of the rose that blooms in front of the porch

The love of my life will be home soon, greeting me with a smile, eyes twinkling, moving in for a kiss hello. He'll taste of sweat, salt, and sawdust from his shop. Our children will see his truck and come running, abandoning their game of chase.

"Daddy, you're home!" They will embrace him with sticky arms and hands. "Look, I skinned my knee!"

I'll have to get up and make dinner soon. We'll eat outside on the big plank table set up in the back. As afternoon turns to dusk, we'll watch the lightning bugs emerge to dance, and listen to the frogs sing their nightly chorus from the creek behind our property. The night blooming flowers will unfold their petals in the soft night air.

A perfect end to a perfect day. A snapshot to memorialize in my heart, savoring every minute.

Note: Kathy has never sat on a porch swing nor seen a lightning bug. But she can imagine.

Prompt: Imagine sitting on a lovely porch. You've been asked to memorize something while sitting on the porch. What do you memorize and why?

What energizes you?

It started with a hummingbird. A wee baby dressed in iridescent green. Too young to fly.

It fell from its nest and landed on my husband's car parked under a tree. He put the baby on the porch where it sat, waiting patiently. Perhaps for its parents who hovered nearby. Perhaps for me to rescue it. When I found it, its entire body was quivering. I could feel its distress. So, I did what I was not supposed to do, although I didn't know it at the time. I made some sugar water and fed it, holding my finger above its beak so the food dripped down my finger. It opened its beak and swallowed over and over until the thimble sized dish of sugar water was gone. It stopped shaking and stepped onto my finger, completely trusting, its eyes on me.

I fell in love with that wee bird. I sang and it chirped as we drove to a bird rescue center. That little hummingbird was so brave. I named it Intrepid. It grew up and was released along with a cohort of other baby hummingbirds who had been rescued at about the same time.

Intrepid led me to the bird rescue center. Now I volunteer there. I prepare meals for sick and injured birds. I hand feed baby birds, enticing them to open their beaks so I can push a syringe full of nourishment into their crops. Baby finches flock to my hand, fighting over who gets the next syringe full of food. Baby woodpeckers climb all around my arm while I try to angle my wrist to shove mealworms into their open beaks. Baby towhees turn their backs and dance from foot to foot, flirting with the syringe until I pick them up, one at a time, to feed them. They are all so small and innocent and in need of care.

I feed and handle the raptors who live at the center. The residents all have some sort of injury that prevents them from being successful in the wild. Now they have jobs as ambassadors for their species. We present them to visitors and teach people how important it is to protect them and their habitats.

I still get an adrenaline rush when I walk with a hawk tethered to my gloved fist. My favorite hawk is wild and feral. Scanning the meadow, she tries to take flight, but being tethered to my fist, she can only circle my hand and step back up. Occasionally she misses my fist and lands on my arm above the glove. My arm is dotted with scars from her talons. When I walk with her, I imagine myself soaring over fields surveying the world from above.

Sometimes in the late afternoon I walk with a great horned owl. As the shadows lengthen, she notices everything, swiveling her head to look behind her. She's content to sit on my fist and watch leaves rustling, songbirds flying, squirrels chasing each other around a tree. I feel regal walking with her.

I hold quail gizzards and intestines in my outstretched hand and wait for a turkey vulture to gently pick up the slimy treats with her beak. She doesn't bite. What a thrill.

Before Intrepid led me to the bird rescue center, I was floundering. I had lost my identity as a working professional. I no longer knew my purpose in life. I didn't know how to be retired. These birds have opened up something in me. They are teaching me how to be in the moment, to reach my calm center. I had no idea that Intrepid would lead me to a place that brings me such joy.

It started with a hummingbird. Now I walk with hawks. I rescued one bird. Several have rescued me.

Kathy Guthormsen

Growing up in Skagit Valley, Washington with its verdant farmland gave Kathy an appreciation for the promise and beauty of nature's bounty. The Cascade and Olympic mountain ranges and old growth forests offered the magic of things unseen and fostered her fertile imagination.

Kathy's work has been published in *The Write Spot: Memories*, *The Write Spot: Possibilities*, and *The Write Spot: Writing as a Path to Healing*. Her Halloween story, *Run*, was published in the Petaluma Argus Courier in October 2020.

When she isn't writing, Kathy volunteers at the Bird Rescue Center in Santa Rosa, California, working with and presenting resident raptors as part of their education and outreach program. Walking around with a hawk or an owl on her fist is one of her favorite pastimes.

Kathy lives in northern California with her husband, one psychotic cat, a small flock of demanding chickens, and a pond full of peaceful koi. She maintains a blog: www.kathyg.space where she occasionally posts essays, short stories, and fairy tales.

Lynn Levy

Summertime

Summer hummed. The slow rise and fall of cicada calls wandered around the horizon. Cicadas were everywhere, but they always sounded far off, lost in echoes.

Angeline sat in cut-off shorts and a tank top, dangling her feet off the upstairs deck. There wasn't any railing. This was in the days long before people won lawsuits for being stupid, so if anyone had walked off the edge and broken a leg, *they'd* have apologized to Angeline's folks for putting them to the trouble of driving them all the way to Clarkson to get it set.

Angeline was skinny as a stick. Mama caller her skinny-mini, and her brother Jack called her a praying mantis—because boys loved bugs and insults, and both at once was a bonus.

But Petey Dawson called her Angel, and blushed like it meant something.

Most days in summer were slow, but in a good way. Angeline would sit still, letting time wash on by. Sometimes she felt like she could hear it babbling clear as any brook, but when she focused in on it, it was just the cicadas, passing the call around and around.

The air was heavy and lush and full of green smells, and the adults all talked about the humidity and being sticky and moaned and complained, but Angeline felt like she'd only just gotten warm enough. That was summer—warm air on bare legs and her hair tickling her back and fifteen cents in her pocket for soft-serve later, when the fireflies came out, glittering and lighting her path, and giving way to stars as the moon rose, just like the cicadas gave way to crickets and frogs.

Summer sang to Angeline. Winter was a dense hush, a white blankness like the snow, barely broken by the crackle of a fire or the ping of the pipes or the hiss of the radiator, all impatience and yearning. Summer was deep and languid. Angeline could disappear into the cicada song like a trance, and did sometimes. But sometimes not.

"Hey, Angel."

Angeline opened her eyes and looked down on Petey. He blushed. He always blushed.

"What's up, Petey?"

"Wanna walk to the reservoir?"

Angeline considered it for a second—the way the woods would smell, the feeling of leaf duff around her feet. The mud between her toes. The cool water closing around her like a sleeve.

"Uh huh," she said. She jumped down to the ground, a solid ten feet, folded, rolled, and stood up.

"Gonna break your neck someday," Petey said.

"Not today, though," Angeline answered.

Petey Dawson lived six houses down, and they'd been playing together since they were kids. They knew each other's freckles and scars and which parents said yes more to their own kids, and which more to someone else's. They got put on projects together at school, and were allowed to run wild in summer as long as the grownups knew they were together.

"C'mon," Angeline said. Now that she was down, she was itching to move.

"Huh," Petey said, and had to run a few strides to catch up.

You couldn't hear the cicadas so much in the woods, but you heard birds, their clear, high fluting, their chirps and chatter, and still with that summertime echo, like the sound of it was bouncing between all the leaves. It was cooler, too. The air felt thinner and richer all at the same time. Mrs. Coluso had taught them about trees making oxygen way back in 3rd grade, and Angeline always thought she could feel it, the good, pure air of the woods, fresh-made.

The white rush of the waterfall was just getting loud enough to hear over the leaves rustling, and bit by bit, as they walked, the two sounds changed places, the water drowning out the rest.

Angeline liked that she and Petey could walk for half an hour and not say anything. She felt him beside her on the path, keeping pace. He'd always been near as skinny as her, but lately he'd been getting taller. It was weird to tip her head up to look at him, but it was something she was getting used to. They scrambled down the bank, using tree roots as steps and grips, and tumbled down the last 10 feet straight into the water.

Petey came up first, his hair plastered to his head, droplets of water making stars that shone and sparkled as they rolled down his face.

Angeline pulled through the current to the center, and came out on the flat rock there.

"C'mon!" she called.

Petey came and sat beside her; two folded figures with crossed arms around bent knees, barefoot, nut-brown, and nothing in front of them but acres of future.

"I love summertime," Angeline said. She felt full up with it.

"I know," Petey said.

Angeline didn't kiss Petey that day, or the one after, or the whole of that summer. But years on down the line, when she remembered, when one of the grandkids asked, Angeline always picked that day as the first one. Because looking at Petey, all angles and elbows and gentle agreement, covered in sparkles and asking nothing, it was the first time she ever thought she might.

Prompt: Poem: Patty's Charcoal Drive-In by Barbara Crooker.

Not at All

Katz scratched his neck, and then held up three fingers.

"That's all?" Jimmy scoffed.

"How many for you, then?" Katz asked.

Jimmy shrugged. "Lost count." Jimmy was Katz's age, but he seemed older. He wasn't bigger, it was just that he carried himself with an ease that made him seem way more than 14.

"You can't name 'em, it didn't happen," Katz said.

"You name yours?" Jimmy asked.

"Polewater Street, Chicago. Drawmore Lane, North Plattsville, and Loukonen Dam Road, Boulder."

"Nice places?" Jimmy asked.

"They were ok," Katz allowed.

"How come you move so much?"

"My dad changes jobs a lot. How come you?"

"My dad's in the army. Was." Jimmy winced a little. "They move you around a lot. The addresses aren't as pretty-sounding, though."

"Miss any of them?" Katz asked.

"I liked the base in California. It was warm there and I could get to the beach on my own. But the apartments were always the same. Once we unpacked, sometimes I'd wake up and forget we moved."

"I miss the Boulder house most, I think," Katz said. "It wasn't the biggest one, but it was the most normal. I actually made friends with the neighbors, kind of." He was quiet for a bit.

"School's hard, though."

"Yeah," Jimmy agreed.

It was what they had in common, the army brat and the CEO's son. Always the new kid. Never anyplace long enough to set roots or make the kind of friends that mattered, the ones you'd still be talking to after high school, the ones that'd be at your wedding, the ones whose kids would call you Uncle someday.

"Why aren't you on a base anymore?" Katz asked. Then he slapped his hand to his mouth.

"Sorry."

"Nah, he didn't die or anything. It's ok. Ma got tired of moving, so he quit the army. But she didn't much like being married to a propane salesman, it turned out, so here we are. She moved back to where her folks are from, and now I got cousins I'm supposed to like."

"What'd they ever do for you?" Katz asked.

"Exactly," Jimmy agreed.

"Tell me the best thing about one of the places you used to live," Katz said.

"You first," Jimmy stalled.

"Well, I know I said Boulder, but the house in Chicago, it was old. Real old. The kind of old where you sort of feel the spirits of other people wandering through. It had a lot of dark wood and huge built-in cabinets I used to make forts out of, they were so big, and a chandelier in the dining room, and stained-glass panels in the ceiling. When I was little, really little, y'know, little enough to like spinning?"

Jimmy nodded.

"I'd spin around in that huge dining room until I was dizzy enough to fall down, and then just stare up through the stained glass. It had a hummingbird. I used to think I could see it moving when I did that, but it was probably just my eyeball juice sloshing around."

Jimmy laughed and Katz felt warm. It was a good laugh, and the first one he'd gotten.

"Your turn," Katz said.

"Best base house was the one in Fort Hood, because it *was* a house, not an apartment. It was tiny—it'd probably fit in that dining room of yours. Twice. It seemed huge though, 'cause I was really small, too. But that's the first time I remember what it was like when my dad came home. I was too young to really remember missing him, but I remember how happy Mom was when he came back. She cooked and baked like a fiend. If I close my eyes I can still remember the smell. She painted the kitchen yellow. She wasn't supposed to, but she did. I think that was my favorite one."

"Ever want to go back?" Katz asked.

"Nah. You?"

"Nah," Katz agreed. He didn't have to ask why not. He'd moved on enough times to know things were different after a spell away. People, too. If you had something warm to remember, it was best not to mess it up with anything real.

Jimmy pulled a pack of smokes out of his pocket, and offered one to Katz.

Katz pulled it free from the others, feeling the slight, papery friction. He'd never held one. There was tiny, crisp writing on the filter. "I don't actually smoke," he said.

Jimmy took it back, and Katz missed the feel of it in his fingers, just for a second.

"Good for you," Jimmy said. "Bad habit." He lit up and took a long drag.

"Mrs. Hapstein will kill you if she catches you."

"Not actually," Jimmy said. And Katz could tell in the

matter-of-fact way he said it, that Jimmy wasn't scared of Mrs. Hapstein, not even a little. It was a point of view Katz had never even considered—a life without fear of grown-ups, of consequences. All at once the idea of being in charge of yourself filled up his whole head, and he was almost as dizzy as he'd been back in the days of the glass dining room hummingbird.

He watched Jimmy smoke the cigarette, the way the tip glowed, the smoke coming out his nose, the languid way he leaned back against the bricks of the school, the practiced flick of his fourth finger knocking off the ash.

Jimmy noticed, and handed it over. "Don't puke," he said.

The smoke burned going in, and it burned coming out, and his eyes watered like he was crying for his momma, but he managed not to cough.

Jimmy laughed again and slapped him on the shoulder. "You'll do," he said, and took back the cigarette.

Katz felt ten feet tall.

Inside the school the last bell rang and they were really out, not just wiling away 7th period study hall. They parted, heading for the houses that kept them each now, in this incarnation of their lives.

The screen door slammed behind Katz when he got home, and there was Mom, looking glamorous and worried.

"Did you make any friends?" she asked.

"Yeah," said Katz.

"Ooh," she beamed. "Will I like him?" she asked.

Katz smiled. "No," he said. "I don't think so. Not at all."

Prompt: Write about a house you no longer go to.

Hercules

Hercules the cat had a penchant for hiding things. But that's the end of the story, and it's usually best to start at the beginning.

In the beginning, Mary wanted a kitten. Ma said no, and Pa said yes, and they had a big fight about it, and Mary was sorry she asked, and tried to say she didn't want a kitten after all, but it didn't fix the cloud in the house, the way the air felt heavy and electric, like just before a storm, but without the nice part after, where it feels light and washed clean, and everything smells good.

Hercules was not a kitten when he arrived. He wasn't old, but he was already big and more than a bit war-torn, with one shredded ear and a kink in his tail, and no whiskers on one side of his face. He was pretty beat up and Ma couldn't stand to see a thing suffer, so after she'd paid the vet to patch him up, she figured on keeping him around to earn his keep by ratting.

Hercules was amenable. Pa managed not to smirk about it. And Mary got the job of nursing him, which made Hercules her cat in no time.

Mary found the first of his stashes when he'd been with them for a year. It was under her dresser. She'd decided to rearrange her room and when she pulled the dresser across the floor there were twist ties and hair ribbons and bottle caps and two of Mom's good earrings and a teaspoon.

Mary never told on Hercules, but she did put the earrings back.

Ma liked jigsaw puzzles, and Hercules liked the card table. But when the puzzle was done, the table went away, and with it, his den. Lately Ma never could seem to finish, though. There was always a piece missing.

Mary knew where they were, every one. But by the time she figured it out, the cloud had come back to stay, and there were days when Hercules seemed like her only friend. So she let him keep them. The last pieces of the puzzles.

Prompt: The last piece of the puzzle.

What energizes you?

This is a hard question. This has always been a hard question. I have never had a singular passion—one thing that made me say, "Yes, that, definitely." I've had more of a "Yeah, that could be cool, for now, maybe," sort of interaction with life.

So, I don't know how to answer.

I like finishing things. I like the satisfaction of crossing things off a list. Though as I move through my 50s, I am beginning to suspect that the whole idea of "getting finished" or even "catching up" is entirely fiction. Somehow, the list never shortens.

I have moments that fill me up, but they are usually unexpected, unplanned, unforeseen. They do not happen when I seek them out, but they sometimes sneak up on me. I recently acquired a new yard with plants that are *not dead* and I'm just tickled by it. I find myself delighted that when you have soil, instead of clay, pulling weeds is easy. Dumb things. Ephemeral things. Passing moments.

I love the ocean and the fog. I used to love the smell of

wood smoke, but after four once-in-a-century wildfires unbearably close to home, I decidedly do not any more.

I don't know. I find this kind of question utterly perplexing. I suppose it's easy for other people to answer. As I was once told, "Not everyone is like you, Lynn."

Sometimes I feel energized. Sometimes I feel dull and exhausted. But I think the stories I tell myself to explain why I'm feeling one or the other are just that. I like many things. I dislike others. But activity and emotion don't correlate reliably. So when you ask me straight out, "What energizes you? What do you want?" my mind goes blank and I can't think of a thing.

Lynn Levy

Lynn Levy has led a few different lives. Starting out as the clichéd, outcast, weird kid in school, she graduated to a collegiate rebirth that involved the novelty of having friends, plural, to being an audio engineer, where she felt excited to be working with cool musicians and cool technology and also terrified of being found out as an uncool fraud, to software engineer, which she found fun, logical, and totally absorbing, to middle management, which she wasn't cut out for, and lately, to technical writer, which she's finding fresh and fantastic.

On the side, she has dabbled with throwing pots, growing tomatoes, playing the drums, and writing fiction. The best part of her journey has been the husband and the friends she picked up along the way.

In her 50s, she is enjoying the feeling of caring a bit less about things that don't matter, and living a bit more, in spite of the lockdown of 2020. She lives in Northern California with her husband, the ghosts of cats, and musings of children running loose in her head.

Carmel Beach

Being the sunset is a moment you surrender to,
Turning gold, pumpkin, fuchsia, awash in deep lavender.
Emerald waves, blind to your movie screen
Soften to foamy pearls over a powdered granite bed.

Being the silken sand, you become a hallowed perch
Molded, custom fit for gluteal divots.
You give in to cold toes burrowing for warmth.
Oversee as chair, preside as dorsal fins pop.

Being the dolphin pod feeding in rich waters,
Arcs of black roll through the drifting eventide.
You boil the ocean's surface, dodging friends,
Your smooth body is liquid joy and power.

Being young again, strong belly lying in the shallows,
Rollers break over your dragged print in the sand
Giggling, orange jewels sparkle on your wet shoulders,
Flat bubble-glass sheets cast you like a bug in amber.

Being the wave, you delight in the life you bring to the land
Effortlessly caressing the slope of beach
Depositing little bits of yourself, leaving
Subtle messages and gifts at dusk before the coming storm.

Being the gathering clouds, you lie across the fringe of darkness
Backlit by a fading orb you shape shift in three dimensions,
Hue and value, line your sharp edges and soft centers.
Being the sunset, you touch the elements,

Regard them all—or maybe just one—aware of being aware.

Prompt: Happiest moment of the week.

Provisions

I gasped with horror as I opened the door to the pantry to find Jif. Jif is what happens when 19-year-old twin boys grocery shop for the family in times of COVID-19. Jif is a "peanut food" with hydrogenated oils—my favorite being rapeseed and I'd like to know what pervert named that—doused with molasses and sugar. Jif is manufactured by science, and so thoroughly processed, that a peanut would not recognize its own name. "Take a whiff of Jif!" was the slogan I grew up with, and as kids, we mocked the motto when something smelled really foul in the bathroom.

My twins also purchased a slew of conventionally grown vegetables rather than organics, which was another disappointment given that I was known to expound on the merits of local and organic while remaining a generally non-militant vegetarian. But hell, they bought VEGETABLES; so, some parenting methodology was sticking.

While I could relinquish organically grown for the pandemic, I was steadfast on the humane treatment of animals. Thankfully, my meat-eating young men grasped this lesson which was proven upon review of the newly-stocked freezer filled with locally farmed and free-range meat. Not bad, boys!

I am aware a mom's quality food benchmark is bound to drop when hungry, fast-paced sons on assignment are magnetized by clever marketing taglines and flashy labeling. My offspring are out on the front lines battling aggressive shoppers who cannot keep their distance or who lazily wear their masks, covering mouths but not noses. Once they are back and washing up the groceries with bleach spray, they are protecting their old mom and dad from an unseen threat. What good boys!

Still, Jif crossed the threshold and pushed the limits on the very definition of peanut butter and what I consider edible, but in comes a memory. The last time I tried Jif was college days when my go-to dinner was Top Ramen and a 7-Eleven hard-boiled egg. I recall Jif's desserty-sweet smoothness. What shifts in my life made me so opposed to a little unhealthy pleasure?

Maybe Jif is just mislabeled or having an identity crisis. Maybe my pre-COVID living standards could adjust a little to relax the hard clamp on ideals. Maybe pride, privilege, and general food snobbery has me in a false tirade for principle over truth. What if I like Jif? If I do, I will not tell my twins.

Prompt: Write about something that is hard to eat.

Color Washed

I use the best black at the edges to ground my paintings with a little gravity, but it doesn't come ready-made from a tube. A complex black is a color made by combining all the pigments in the paint box—foggier than charcoal and ruddier than slate. It's the mix that matters. The blank white page on the table asks to be worked blending intent with abandon. Where do I begin?

A carmine red kayak glides on a lazy day, skimming the brackish salt and fresh liquid mixture in the Petaluma Slough, whose woody peat is easily churned and never settles. In this fluid melting pot, Sonoma Mountain runoff meets jellyfish from Russia. The color of water is frog brown with golden glitter-shimmers that stripe when sliced by ducks and other paddlers. A steel encased canal layered with algae and mud, renders a landscape painted by the rise and fall of the tide. Army engineers erected this flood protection zone so developers could cheaply build housing on adjacent wetlands. A tossed blue blanket, dirty, once wet, lies crumpled on the rocky bank. The boat travels up the slough into the finer watershed where homeless encampments cluster beneath the oaks. Tied with a dirty yellow bungee, a junked tangerine tent pokes through the scrub. Egrets, mallards, and Canadian geese move aside for the lone red boater. The water neither looks nor smells clean, though hydrologists claim it is. Where do those adrift go to go?

The oar cuts silent figure eights; river drips spill down the shaft onto bare thighs. The slough turns to creek, lined with willow, cattails, and bulrush. The craft drifts close to riparian secrets—a sanctuary where birds, fish and otter shelter, and valley oaks cool the pools and soothe celadon borders. Life springs from a coffee tinted rainbow composed in muddy time graphics that line the waterfront where hidden census material embeds. Whoever settles or drifts here owns the place—affordable housing for any to claim. Does the pristine habitat clash with garbage strewn under the trees and the metal channel walls? Or does the mix infuse into a rich complex color field of existence?

The Petaluma Slough is a fluid continuum from ocean, bay, estuary, to tidal slough, river, creek, past brook mouths to Earth-natural. Its passages take the red vessel backwards through eons to fire and rain and lifted continental plates to rich valleys of Sonoma loam washing into the murky downstream flow.

Turning the kayak around, I splash faster past the keen details, paddling back to an old house that holds my color box. My mind has already left the slough, already moved on—eager to paint this alluvial world on paper.

Prompt: Make a list of colors; then write adjectives that start with the same letter as the color.

What energizes you?

Coffee then:
Daybreak, birdsong, and meditation
Heart yoga, tingly Savasana
Morning runs on a broad stretch of beach

Abandon while:
Dancing to good ole funk
Belly laughing with friends
Skiing fresh powder with my sons

Alone time with:
Sierra Nevada Mountains
Granite slabs and a rockbound lake
My dog, swimming together

Crying because:
A book changed my life
My burden is released
It's the perfect movie

That flow state when:
Crafting an art piece
Blasting down a chute
I'm on a deadline

The pure joy of:
Freewriting poems and essays
Lively talks with someone close
Feeling fully alive and robust

M.A. Dooley

In first grade, her family credited her award-winning poem as the start of her writing career, but the following year's poetry experience proved disappointing. Though Dooley was awarded a commendable second place for her poem, she put her pencil down and walked away from writing. This long hiatus began as a result of Dooley's father who, intending to be helpful, strongly suggested she write "joyous" in front of "raindrops." She sensed that his meddling would continue; so she retired at age seven.

Following another career path, Dooley became a licensed architect and runs a design firm in Sonoma County with her architect husband. As a multi-media artist and photographer, Dooley follows creative expressions that nourish her spirit and help her understand life and her mind.

Returning to the page many decades later, Dooley now drains pens onto paper like raindrops joyously drenching parched earth.

Nona Smith

The Year of the Accessory Mask

I celebrated my birthday this year in corona virus lockdown mode. As you might expect, it was a socially distanced, quiet affair. No restaurants were open and it seemed sad to add birthday candles to a dessert when it was just me and my husband Art, celebrating. The birthday cards I received via snail mail were mostly about drinking martinis and cats (my friends know me well) and the presents were viral-themed: beautifully wrapped anti-bacterial soaps, a heavily lavender-scented, just-the-right-size-to-keep-in-the-car hand sanitizer kit and face masks. Which brought my new mandatory accessary to a total of four. Can a girl ever have too many?

I bought my first mask in early February before wearing them was mandated, but after it was apparent they were difficult, if not impossible, to obtain. An entrepreneurial local woman who made lovely lingerie, repurposed her business from undies and bras to mask making. Tiny, very feminine bows hid the stitching that attached the elastic ties to the side of the mask . . . elastic ties that caught my hair in tangles when I put it on and again when I took it off. That, and the fact that it looked like I had an A-cup bra on my face, made me tuck this item away and look for another version.

The second mask came to me by way of the generosity of my neighbor Betty who was turning them out by the dozens and donating them to family, friends, and the local hospital. "Come over and choose one for yourself and one for Art," she said.

Standing the appropriate remoteness from her, I pointed to a lovely floral-print mask displayed on a bench close to her entryway. Eyeing the others and searching for a more masculine design, I selected one in brown tones for Art. Once home, I took a good look at my choice and saw the print was of cute cavorting rodents.

Betty's creations attached the mask to the face with over-the-head, wide elastic bands. Although much better than the first mask . . . in both appearance and comfort . . . the elastic bands were too long to keep it properly in place. It kept creeping up under my eyes and tickling my lower lashes, making it impossible to read my grocery list or see the arrows on the floor pointing the way my cart should be headed.

My sister, who doesn't sew but is a big online shopping fan, came to the rescue with two birthday present masks. Both have comfortable behind-the-ear attachments, but I need to be careful taking them off to make sure my expensive hearing aids don't slip off with them. One mask is cotton and in my favorite shades of green. The other—the one that fits me best—is crocheted. I'm a bit concerned about the holes in this mask making it a less protective device. And it does tickle my nose after a while . . . and I do tend to get over-heated wearing it. But still, it stays properly in place, doesn't tangle my hair and doesn't look like a bra.

With so little else to occupy me, I admit I've spent several hours on the computer, checking out more options. It seems that in the past two months an entire cottage industry has sprung up around masks. They are made from various kinds of materials in every color and pattern imaginable: paisley bandanas that stagecoach robbers used to wear and masks resembling Darth Vader, masks made out of yarmulkes, and others out of LED rechargeable, glow-in-the-dark lights. I found a variety pack of masks with different smiling faces, so a person could conceivably display their mood on any given day and yet remain socially distanced.

My favorite—to date—is the "bead-fringed, multi-functional neck gaiter" which does double duty, allowing its wearer to act as a responsible masked citizen in public while it converts into an elegant accessory scarf with a little tuck maneuver when visiting within one's sanctioned social pod.

During these weeks and months of lockdown, when it seems our whole way of life has eroded, I've managed to avoid spending a great deal of time wondering (read "worrying") about the future. We're in unknown territory, and I can't begin to imagine what life post-COVID-19 will look like. I'm hoping that we'll be able to return to socializing mask-free. I like to imagine that sometime in the not-too-distant future, a young child will come across a stash of masks and wonder what they were used for. I'm wishing that when this curious child is told, "They were supposed to keep us from spreading a dangerous virus," that child won't snicker the way we now do when we remember how sheltering under our school desks and covering heads with our arms was supposed to protect us from atomic fallout.

Prompt: Write about a favorite accessory.

Nona Smith

And Then There's the Gratitude List

I'm a list maker. I believe they keep my life orderly. I have a list for grocery shopping, one for birthdays, and To Do, Worry, and Frustration lists. The latter consists of stuff I haven't yet figured out how to deal with. Recently I created a Gratitude List.

I know this last one sounds strange, given we're into the eighth month of a global pandemic—and the sixth month of taking it seriously. COVID-19 has been identified and YouTube has a million visuals of what it looks like. So far, there's no cure for it, but there are ways to prevent its spread and most of us can recite those in our sleep: wash your hands as though you've been trained by Lady Macbeth, keep a six-foot distance from anyone not living in your house, wear a mask.

So much has changed since this time last year. In 2019, few of us had any idea who Dr. Anthony Fauci was. By 2020, however, he's become a household name, a truth-telling superhero. We're now familiar with creative ways to Shelter in Place and have recovered from our need to hoard toilet paper. Most of us are no longer obsessed with daily statistics about where the virus is peaking and how many people have died on any given day, although newspaper and TV broadcasting is all about that. That, and sports events where games are played in empty stadiums with simulated fans and pre-recorded cheering. Life, as we knew it, is very different this year.

But I've got to admit—with no small amount of guilt—that so far, my husband and I have not been greatly affected by the changes this virus has wrought. No one we know and love has gotten sick from it. We live in a small rural community where neighbors look out for each other, and the incidence of the virus has been very low. Art and I are retired, so we haven't lost jobs. We know where our next meal and mortgage payments are coming from. We're especially grateful that we have no young children living with us who we're responsible for educating and entertaining 24/7. Truth is, we've actually come to appreciate the slower pace this time has imposed upon us. We're lucky, and we know it.

Hence, the creation of the Gratitude List.

Which is not to say this lockdown time has been a cake walk. There are distressing issues that have arisen for me during it. Close to the top of that list is social distancing: asking our son, and my sister who live in another part of the state, not to visit; not being able to hug my friends. Elbow bumping is a poor substitute for a pulling-someone-close hug. And two-dimensional Zooming lacks the intimacy of an in-person conversation.

But the item that tops my Frustration List is masks. Don't get me wrong: I own several and don them religiously when I go out in public. I appreciate that others wear them as well, and don't feel my First Amendment rights are being infringed upon in the least. So, what's my issue? My issue is, I'm hard of hearing. When people have their masks properly in place, I become socially isolated.

My hearing aids, which I wear all the time, work . . . to a point. But I depend heavily upon lip reading as well. This masking business, besides muffling words, makes it impossible for me to see anyone's lips. It's not only a frustration for me and the people I'm interacting with, but I'm also concerned it might be a danger.

Last week, for instance, I went grocery shopping and picked up a copy of the San Francisco Chronicle for Art who prefers those crossword puzzles over the easier ones in the *Press Democrat.* I placed the paper on the conveyer belt along with my other groceries, and when the clerk came to it, she held it up and asked me something. Behind her mask, her words were distorted and I had no visual cues to guess what she was saying.

"Excuse me?" I said.

She repeated the question.

Again, sounds came out of her mouth, passed through the mask and were garbled beyond my recognition. I shook my head, gestured to my ears and asked her, apologetically, to repeat herself once more.

This time, she leaned forward to the protective plexiglass screen that separated us and said whatever she said for the third time. And for the third time, I couldn't make out a word of it. Not wanting to try her patience further, I smiled and nodded my head in what I hoped was an appropriate response. It wasn't until I got home and handed the folded paper to Art that I understood her question.

Holding the *Chronicle* aloft, with a copy in each hand, Art asked, "And was there a reason you bought two of them?"

Okay, so this is a mildly amusing episode. But this is just one example of many mildly amusing interactions I've had lately. And when one mildly amusing incident piles on top of another mildly amusing incident, they become a lot less amusing. I begin to worry about what important things I might miss. Perhaps something that would put someone in danger or otherwise harm or inconvenience them. And then I begin to wonder if this item belongs on my Worry

List instead of the Frustration List. Or maybe it belongs on both of them.

Before I get myself too worked up, I return to my Gratitude List and take a breath. No one we care about has contracted the virus. We're healthy, well-fed and not concerned about money. We live in a beautiful, caring community and aren't responsible for young children. I pick up my pen and add to the list my gratitude for family and friends who are patient with me and willingly repeat things for the fourth time, who face me when they speak, who don't start a conversation from another room or while their head is in the refrigerator. So what if I buy two newspapers? My Gratitude List is still longer than my Frustration List.

Prompt: Lists.

Nona Smith

The Trap or What I Did While Sheltering in Place

July 2020, four months into sheltering in place.

My husband Art and I were living in a state of malaise. We'd cleaned out drawers and cupboards and closets and even tackled the garage. With our freezer still chock full of hearty homemade soups and comfort food casseroles I made in the early days of SIP, I'd stopped cooking. We'd become very adept at our newly acquired skill of Zooming and gotten quite good at figuring out obscure crossword puzzle clues. But we hadn't been drawn to do the very things that nurtured our creativity before COVID-19 struck. The only time since February Art spent in his jewelry studio was to tidy it up. And my writing muse seems to have chosen somewhere else to shelter in place. So, Art and I began wishing for a distraction, something to occupy our lockdown days.

However, when it turned up, we weren't so pleased.

"Oh, no," I cried.

My plaintive wail brought Art to my side his face creased in concern. "What? What's wrong?"

I pointed out the window toward our backyard. "Just look at that."

He shifted his gaze from me to the window, and I could tell from the questioning expression on his face that what he saw wasn't registering. And then it was.

"Wow," he said in his characteristically calm voice.

"Crap," I said, not quite so calm.

Together we walked outside to survey the damage. What yesterday was a large swath of lush groundcover, this morning was pure upheaval. Verdant plants had been ripped from the ground, their white roots exposed in a tangle, their tiny buttercup-like flowers matted. The sight made me tearful. I dropped to my knees and began to press the salvageable plants back into the earth and put aside the ones that clearly were no longer viable. When I was done, a disturbing amount of brown dirt was visible between the plants. I hand watered the area, the hose on the gentlest nozzle setting I could select.

"We can replant this," Art said. I could tell he was trying to lift my spirits. "Let's go to the nursery."

"We're not replanting until we find out who did this," I said. My dander was up.

We spent the afternoon canvassing our neighbors. Had they experienced such destruction in their yards? Reports of visitations abounded: long-eared hares, whole skunk families, deer that jumped fences and ate everything in sight, elegant grey foxes, ugly pink-nosed possums, a sleek weasel, and, of course, raccoons. One neighbor complained bitterly about a lumbering, stubby-tailed raccoon who dug under his fence and attempted to get into his henhouse. But no reports of damage like ours.

Our friend Donald offered to install his night camera to spy on the nocturnal activity in our yard while we slept. He strapped the camera to a thick stake which he placed in the area where the destruction had occurred. In the early morning, he retrieved it and watched the film on his computer.

"It's a stubby-tailed, limping old raccoon," he reported.

Aha! We identified our culprit. Now we needed to figure out what to do about him.

One neighbor suggested we call Animal Control.

"How do they work?" Art asked.

"They bring a trap, set it up, and then you call them when you've caught something. They'll get rid of it for you."

"Get rid of it how?"

"They take it away."

"And . . . do what with it?" Art persisted.

"Well . . . they destroy it. Drown it or shoot it or something."

Our eyes got wide. While I wanted to wring this animal's neck for what it had done to our garden, I didn't want to set a hit man on him. (I was convinced it was a him.)

"You can borrow our Havahart trap," our friend Les offered. "It traps the animal without harming it, and you can drive it away to some distant location in the forest and release it there."

This sounded like a better plan to us.

The following day, Les arrived with a metal contraption the size of a large duffle bag. He set it down in the now almost-barren part of our garden and showed us how to set the trap. "Put the bait behind this metal plate, and it will trigger the door shut when the critter steps on it."

He handed us a can of fish-flavored cat food whose "use by" date was long past and said to call him when we trapped something. "I'll help you relocate it."

And so, the saga began.

At nightfall, I peeled back the top of the cat food can and placed it where Les instructed. I checked on the trap four or five times before we went to bed, but there was nothing to see, no raccoon in sight.

Early the next morning, I bounded down the stairs to see what we'd captured. To my great disappointment, I found nothing more than the cat food inside the cage.

"We'll put something else in for bait tonight," Art said.

That immediately set me to thinking about what might be more tempting than an old can of mackerel. That evening, just after sunset, I added two prawns from our dinner to the cat food can. I pushed them through the wire mesh and they landed on top of the mackerel. While I didn't want to shoot or drown this animal, I wasn't above poisoning him.

On Day Three, I roused myself early and loped downstairs, hoping for a better result than we'd had on Day Two. But no, the cat food and the prawns were untouched. I tipped the cage over and shook out the bait. Frustrated, I considered meal planning with more inspiration.

Our neighbors had helpful suggestions: peanut butter, bacon, fresh fruit, trail mix. "Set out a path of nuts leading into the cage," someone offered.

That night, I placed a leftover falafel behind the trigger mechanism and scattered a few grapes and almonds around the opening and well into the cage. That should do it, I thought.

I woke late on Day Four. Leaving Art in bed, I ambled downstairs to see what we'd captured.

Squinting out the window, I couldn't believe what I saw. I went outside for a closer look. The cage was still set, but all the goodies I'd left—including the falafel—were gone. Upon closer inspection, I noticed a hole had been dug in the dirt under one corner of the trap. Some critter had outsmarted us, rooted under the cage, and helped itself to the treats by reaching between the metal bars.

"Tonight," I told Art with great determination, "we're moving the trap to the gravel path. Let's see him dig under *that.*"

That night, I set the trap with peanut butter. I dropped a big dollop of it directly onto the metal strip that triggered the door closed. Added to that, I folded a piece of raw bacon and secured it to the top of the cage with a twisty tie where it dangled down just over the metal trigger. Then I fashioned a Hansel and Gretel-like grape trail into the trap.

"There, *that* should do the trick for sure," I said with satisfaction.

Donald offered to set up his camera again so we could view the capture on video. I could hardly wait until morning.

Day Five: Amazing. Some animal was industrious enough to dig under the gravel *and* the cloth beneath it to get at the food. Not a scrap of bacon was left, although the twisty tie was still in place. The grapes were gone and so was the peanut butter. Film from the night camera showed a large skunk working industriously at dislodging the bacon with his dexterous claws and reach in through the metal bars to get at the peanut butter, navigating around the metal trigger.

More than a little annoyed that we with college educations were being out-foxed by a wild thing, our determination to rid our garden of marauding pests hardened. Tonight, we would fool-proof the cage. Tonight, we would move it to cement.

When night fell, with the cage firmly settled on a cement slab, I baited it with another piece of tied-on bacon, some bits of cheese I forced through the top of the trap near the trigger, and a trail of fresh fruit salad: peach and apple slices and some chunks of pineapple.

Day Six: Success! But not in the form we hoped for. A large and ugly possum was pacing the cage nervously when we came downstairs. Back and forth, back and forth he strode. We draped a tarp over the cage, hoping that would calm him while we decided what to do with him. Being raised in big cities, this was honestly the first time we'd considered how we'd actually handle whatever we trapped.

We remembered Les' generous offer to call him for help, but before we called him, we decided to find out more about what possums ate. This guy wasn't the culprit who destroyed our garden and we didn't want to punish him if he'd done nothing wrong. And sure enough, Googling possums, we discovered they are marsupials who prefer moles, voles, and gophers over grubs.

"Let's let him go," Art said.

I was in agreement and removed the tarp to open the cage, getting closer to the possum than either he or I felt comfortable about. He opened his mouth—giving me an up-close look at his many sharp teeth—and he hissed at me! We backed away from each other. Shaken, I went inside, leaving Art and Donald (who appeared at this fortuitous moment to collect his camera) to deal with setting the critter free.

On the Seventh Day we rested. We didn't set the trap. Instead, we watched a young fox nap in our backyard. We admired a doe and her spotted fawn nibble the heather in our front yard.

But by Day Eight, we were back at it.

It would be an exaggeration to say I spent the day designing a nourishing menu for the stubby-tailed varmint. Of course, I didn't. But I'll admit to having him in mind when I cleaned out the refrigerator. In the produce drawer, I found a limp carrot and an over-ripe peach. I tucked these into a plastic bag to which I added the remaining grapes. In another drawer, there were bits and pieces of unidentifiable cheese growing green mold. Those too went into the bag. Way in the back of the third shelf, I discovered a jar of gefilte fish with one piece missing. Obviously from a Passover past and a testament to how fond we are of gefilte fish. I tossed the jar into the garbage, figuring the raccoon wouldn't like its contents any more than the rest of us. I labeled the bag "raccoon food," so Art would know this wasn't for snacking, and put the lot back in the fridge. Before going to bed, I carefully loaded the trap, being sure to place the cheese and produce well beyond the metal set plate. For good measure, I added a dollop of peanut butter to the mix. It looked tempting to me. I only hoped the raccoon would feel the same way.

Day Nine. *Something* appreciated the meal I'd prepared the previous night. When I came downstairs on this morning, I found the cage empty. Not only was there no trapped animal, there was not a morsel of food left. Not even a single grape. And yet . . . the door to the trap was un-sprung. How could that possibly be?

Donald had the answer on video which he gallantly emailed to me without comment.

On screen, I watched myself mashing cheese pieces, one after another, through the grilling at the top of the cage, tossing the carrot and peach slices in after it. I took my time laying a grape trail into the trap. But the one thing I forgot to do, the one highly embarrassing thing captured on video, was how I forgot to actually set the trap. The rest of the film was a parade of animals—a skunk, two teenage raccoons, and old Stubby Tail himself—stopping in for a leisurely snack. Smack my head.

On the evening of Day Nine, I drank less wine with our evening meal and set the trap more mindfully, this time baiting it with the skin from our salmon dinner. Do raccoons like salmon, I wondered as I tied the skin onto the trap with the twisty tie left over from Day Four. Or was that bears? I took my chances, thinking if we caught a bear, it would be a small one, given the size of the trap.

Day Ten: Ta-da! We caught a raccoon. Not THE raccoon, but a younger version with a handsome tail. He'd eaten everything in the cage, including the salmon, and was peering out through the wire in what I imagined was a how-do-I-get-out-of-here look. Even though this wasn't the guy who destroyed our garden, he had garden destroying potential and we didn't want to take any chances, so we called Les for his assistance in relocating him.

Art and Les drove this guy, who they guessed weighed in at around thirty pounds, to a wooded area five miles away and released him there. "He didn't give us a backwards glance," Art said. "Just took off into the forest."

Our enthusiasm for this trapping business was waning and we decided to take the next couple of nights off. But by Day Thirteen, we were ready to try again. Either that or return the cage to Les, defeated.

On the evening of Day Thirteen, before dark, I set the trap with bacon again, using the still-attached twisty tie. I let the bacon dangle from the top of the cage, positioning it just above the metal strip. To that, I added a handful of mixed nuts and some slightly stale gluten-free crackers.

Several times before heading for bed, I turned on the deck light, hoping to see some action in the trap. Once, I caught sight of the two teenage raccoons we'd seen on Donald's camera (or raccoons that looked just like them) sniffing around. But as soon as the backyard light went on, they scampered under the deck and out of sight. I was hoping we wouldn't catch them.

Our two cats usually share our bed, but on the morning of Day Fourteen, no cats were around when we woke. When we went downstairs, we saw why. Both cats were standing at the French door leading out to our deck and the cement pad where the trap was located, their noses pressed to the glass. One of the teenage raccoons was inside the cage, his sibling pacing nervously outside it, seemingly looking for a way to break his bro out.

Art and I exchanged sad faces. "We can't relocate him," I said.

"No," Art agreed. "We won't break up a family."

Maneuvering around our cats, we stepped outside. As we approached the cage, the free raccoon scampered under our deck. Art gently tipped the cage onto one end in the hope that the raccoon inside would stay at the bottom of it while I put my hand into the cage and unhooked the complicated double trap door. As I was doing this, I tried hard not to think about a raccoon's ability to climb. As soon as we righted the cage, he too scampered under the deck. Our hope was that both raccoons would be grateful and not grow up to be garden-wrecking adults.

This project was not going as smoothly as we'd envisioned. So far, we'd caught two raccoons and a possum, but not the critter we were specifically after. Still, we weren't ready to give up quite yet.

I set the trap again on nights fourteen, fifteen and sixteen, but the food was there on all three mornings and Donald's camera showed no nighttime activity. Strange. Were they over us? Was the food better somewhere else? I was almost (but not quite) feeling insulted.

On the evening of Day Seventeen, we tried again. Someone had suggested we give the bacon another go, but this time, wrap it tightly in cheesecloth and attach it above the metal strip, close to the top of the cage. The twisty tie was still there, and I was getting very adept at securing things with it. We laid down a trail of mixed nuts into the cage and scattered a bit of fruit on the metal, then went to bed.

Day Eighteen, early morning: Oy. The thing I was most worried about happened. We caught a skunk. A small, double-striped skunk was curled up asleep in the cage when I looked outside. The food was gone, the cheese cloth shredded, the bacon missing, and a skunk was inside the cage, napping in the morning sun. I watched it for a while, hoping to see it breathing, hoping it was only napping and hadn't choked to death on the cheese cloth. Gingerly, I opened the door and stepped out onto the deck. The skunk stirred, raised his pointy head and shifted position.

I didn't feel threatened, but I wasn't going to take any chances. I went into the garage and pulled down a large plastic tarp. Moving slowly and quietly I crept up to the cage and draped the tarp over it. I was hoping the skunk would appreciate being out of the sun and feel less anxious for whatever was going to happen next.

I waited for Art to join me so we could discuss this. Neither of us had any experience dealing directly with a skunk, and we hadn't actually made a plan for capturing one. All I was sure of was I didn't want to transport one in our new car. Or in our old car for that matter. We would have to let him go.

As before, we tipped the cage, opened the door, and stepped back. Way back. But the skunk didn't immediately appear. We waited, shook the cage a little, but neither of us was eager to put our heads down and peer into it to see what was going on. Finally, the skunk waddled out, and taking his own sweet time, he shuffled under the deck, and like the others, disappeared.

"What do you think? Shall we keep trying to catch the stubby tailed guy?" Art asked.

I shrugged. We were in the sixth month of sheltering in place. What else did we have to do?

This was beginning to look like a catch and release project. We were amateurs, sure, but amateurs with college degrees. We should be able to do better than this.

"Have any more bacon?" Art asked. I assumed he was talking about setting the trap again, but no. He was inquiring about breakfast.

On the evening of Day Nineteen, Donald set up his camera and I baited the trap with trail mix and leftover pieces of adobo chicken. I had rinsed the spicy sauce off the chicken, just in case old Stubby Tail didn't like spicy food and tore it into small pieces that I set at the very back of the cage, beyond the metal plate. I made certain to set the trap door and went to bed.

Day Twenty, morning: all the food, including the chicken, was gone, the trap un-sprung. What the heck?

Donald had already been by to pick up his camera, so we checked our email and, sure enough, the answer was there. Art and I watched the video three or four times, not believing what we were seeing. First, a skunk waddled by and nibbled on the items outside the cage. And then old Stubby Tail appeared. He stood erect, sniffed the top of the cage, and cautiously entered. He ate what was in front of the metal trigger. Then, he got down on his knees—who knew raccoons have knees?—crawled to the part of the cage just before the metal plate, reached *over* the plate, and helped himself to the adobo chicken. When he finished eating, he backed out (still on his knees) and lumbered away.

It's clear this raccoon knew more than we did about survival. It's also clear Art and I were never going to capture him. We returned the trap to Les, and after tacking down plastic covering, we replanted our garden. We cut holes in the plastic and dug just deep enough for the plants to go into the ground. Then we covered the plastic with two inches of wood chips. We're hoping old Stubby Tail leaves our new garden alone. But just in case, we have the phone number of Animal Control posted near our phone.

And now we're back to square one, wishing for a new distraction to occupy our lockdown days. Only this time, keeping in mind that old adage "Be careful what you wish for," we'll be more specific about our desires. We don't want just any old thing to turn up.

Prompt: I could never have predicted . . .

What energizes you?

Pre-COVID lots of stuff energized me: creative writing, having friends over for dinner, gardening, reading, cooking, craft projects, social events, volunteering. I could go on. But now? Nothing much stirs my energy.

For the first few weeks that sheltering in place was strongly suggested—but not yet mandated—my husband and I stayed close to home, shopped during old folks shopping hours, stayed away from face-to-face contact with family and friends, and generally took a step back from life as we'd known it. It seemed like the whole world was taking a time out, the earth had stopped spinning and had somehow slipped off its axis.

In the early weeks of SIP, we slept late, went to bed early and some days took a nap in between. We were living the life of sloths. Sadly, the very things that had sustained our creativity pre-COVID, weren't beckoning us now. Art was not in his studio creating beautiful pieces of jewelry. I couldn't find a subject I was interested in writing about. Certainly nothing humorous, which is usually the slant my writing takes.

But as the weeks turned into months, we began to emerge from the gauzy cocoon we'd enveloped ourselves in and little by little accepted that this was our new reality. For how long? Who knows? But we are alive and healthy and together. The sun rises every day, giving us the opportunity to take a breath, to share a tasty meal, to appreciate our companionable cats and check in with our family and friends, to bite into a ripe summer fruit and use our legs to walk our neighborhood. And, yes, to smell the flowers.

Once we accepted that life itself is a blessing, even under these very strange and scary circumstances, we've come to view each day with renewed energy and appreciation. I'm writing again. Art is working on a design for a new ring. We're taking one day at a time and valuing each one.

Nona Smith

Nona Smith discovered her love of writing at an early age when she took a journalism course in junior high. But it wasn't until almost sixty years later, when she and her husband, Art, retired and moved to the Mendocino Coast, that she fully immersed herself in the writing community and felt comfortable calling herself a writer.

At a friend's urging, Nona signed up for a creative writing class at the local community college and later joined a weekly writing group (now in its eighth year.)

For the past decade, Nona has served on the Board of the Mendocino Coast Writers' Conference and is editor of the annual anthology produced by the Writers of the Mendocino Coast, a chapter of the California Writers Club.

She is the author of *Stuffed: Emptying the Hoarder's Nest* (available at Amazon) and numerous short stories and poems that have found their way into various publications including the *Miami Times Herold*.

Once Upon a House

We wish on our birthday candles, on the first evening star, on a four-leaf clover, and how many of those come true?

You can wish for things to be better, to be different, to be other than they are, but like hope, a wish is not a strategy.

But I'm not here to badmouth wishes.

Annie was surprised when, at age 55, she found herself wishing she owned a house. Her own home. She had never been particularly attached to that idea. She had moved around a lot in her life. Not a lot like an Army brat. Not like moving every few months because the checks were going to start bouncing again. More like moving to new student housing every semester of college and law school; like changing jobs every four years trying to find one that didn't leave her hating the law; like moving every few years to flee Northern California's rising rents. She was fine with her rental homes. She scoffed when her house-owning friends bemoaned insurance costs and new roofs and unexpected repairs.

Then suddenly, as the century turned and the towers fell, she began to wish for her own home. She started saying it out loud to her friends. I want to buy a house. They laughed. Everyone knew how hard that was to do in the Bay Area, especially for a single-income household with zero balance in the savings account.

Then one of her friends gave her a house for her birthday. You want a house, Ellen said, here it is. It was a piece of metal art to hang on the wall—a tall skinny house of blue, yellow, and magenta stripes, with a sun, or maybe a full moon, shining down on it. Annie laughed. It was perfect. She hung it on the wall of her rental.

~

Some time passed, and her beloved 103-year-old grandmother, who had lived alone on the farm until she was 98, died. Annie inherited what would have been her mother's share of the farmland, had she not died at age 34 of viral encephalitis. One thousand acres, give or take, of prime Illinois farmland. Her aunts and uncle bought her out. Annie had cash. Enough for a substantial down payment and more.

Annie and her neighbor, Sage, had taken walks for years through the quaint west side neighborhoods of her picturesque former farm town north of San Francisco. Annie would wish she lived in one of the charming cottages that had sprung up there like mushrooms. There was one place they always stopped. Where a small creek emerged from a culvert under a driveway and carried on to the Petaluma River, a large old buckeye tree presided. Annie and Sage couldn't pass by without stopping to address the tree, admire it, talk to it, pat its bark.

With her inheritance in her bank account, Annie began to look at HOUSE FOR SALE ads in the newspaper. She hardly believed she was doing it, but she was. She hardly believed she had a financial planner, a real estate agent, a mortgage broker, and knew exactly how much house she could afford, but she did.

Finally, she was ready to look at houses. One morning an ad caught her eye. The house was her size, her price, and in one of those neighborhoods she and Sage walked. She drove over, getting a little lost because the street didn't go through, so she pulled into the last driveway and identified her destination as the house next door, at the other terminus of the street, which was split by a creek and—the buckeye tree!

"It's the buckeye tree house!" she shouted to no one as she leapt out of the car, leaving it sit in the neighbor's driveway. She walked past a tall hedge and stood in the driveway with a creek running underneath, looking at a house she had never noticed in all the times she and Sage had passed by, having always been focused on the tree. A yellow house, with a blue door, and a magenta brick walkway.

Annie called her real estate agent. "Ray, I found a house. I want to see it now."

It was only its second day on the market, Ray discovered. He'd contact the listing agent. Several days later, they walked through. Annie was charmed. The hardwood floors, the fireplace, the skylights in the big airy kitchen, the guest room with bath *en suite*, the French doors onto a deck and back yard. Everything she had ever wished for and more.

"I want it," she told Ray.

"Look," he said, "it just went on the market. You can't pay asking price. We need to wait. You need to look at other houses so you know your options." She reluctantly agreed. He was the professional.

He showed her a few other houses. She didn't even need to go inside to know she didn't want them. Weeks went by, becoming months, and still the price did not drop. She tried to be patient. She kept walking by what she now called HER house, sometimes with Sage, sometimes not, to see for herself that the FOR SALE sign was still there. One day she felt familiar enough to go through the side gate to the back yard. She stood on the deck and talked to the house. I love you, she said, you are mine. She began going almost every day, sitting on the deck, imagining strings from her heart wrapping around the house.

Annie knew that wishes were like spells. You wove an intention, laid down a track for the Universe to follow. She was weaving a spell on this house. Binding it to her. Putting the Universe on notice.

One day, on a whim, she tried the handle of the French door and it opened. She stepped inside. She walked to each corner of the house: the East/Air, the dining room; the South/Fire, the office; the West/Water, her bedroom; the North/Earth, the living room; the Center/Spirit, the kitchen. She thanked her grandmother, grandfather, mother, father, all those ancestors before her who had worked the land that had transmuted into the money in her bank. She called on the Goddess to make it hers. So mote it be.

The next weekend there was an open house. She went with Ray, who had become a little frustrated at her blowing off his suggestions of other properties to look at. When they entered, there were four couples milling about, oohing and aahing. She grabbed Ray's arm and pulled him out to the front porch.

"There are people in my house, Ray! I want it NOW."

"Ok, ok, quiet, you can't look too eager." He led her away from the door. "I'll make an offer $10,000 below asking."

"Whatever," she said. "I'll pay what they want. I want it now. This is my house."

And so it was. And the first thing she placed in it, once she had the keys and legitimate right to enter, was the little skinny house that Ellen had given her for her birthday those years ago. With the yellow stripes that matched the color of this house, the blue stripes that matched the front door, and the magenta stripes that matched the front porch tiles.

Blessed Be!

Prompt: Wishes.

Patricia Morris

Enough

I sit at a long dining table that looks like a tornado came through and deposited reams of paper and books and random objects—pens, a stapler, Kleenex, a small purse I haven't carried out of the house for 48 days, a half-read newspaper. Nothing seems to get finished. Most of the paper is recipes, and there is actually an order to them. I started, days ago, to sort my piles of recipes—some torn from magazines or newspapers, some printed on 8 ½ x 11-inch computer paper, some scrawled on scraps of note paper. Some of them are stacked into preliminary categories. But this project, like so many others, stalled out, as something else came along to capture my meager attention.

Now I need a file box, and a simple task like running to Staples or Target—probably both because the first one won't have the right size or right color or be made of materials that please me—has become an ordeal. Even a simple shopping excursion requires a mask, a wait in line to get inside the store, another to check out, and carries an underlying fear that everything I touch carries droplets of COVID-19. Even so, I can't seem to stop fiddling with my mask or touching my face, and I'm terribly deficient at cleaning surfaces at home. If this virus wants me, it will have plenty of opportunities to come for me.

What is my instrument of grace in all this? How do I ground into my patience?

Sitting in meditation and imagining that each out breath could be my last. Wandering my small back yard and taking in the pale blue clouds of forget-me-nots that just appeared on their own several years ago and expand their area every year. Discovering the first sweet, white mock orange blossoms hiding behind the green leaves. Pondering the Buddhist slogan: "Turn all difficulties into the Path."

My sangha is studying the Paramita of Patience. Patience begins with having patience with oneself. Meaning, don't beat myself up for not yet getting back to the recipe project. Trust that its time will come. Patience with the friend who snaps at me out of her frustration with the process of filing for self-employed unemployment compensation. Patience with my computer hard drive, that chose this critical time to crash, leaving me not knowing what writing or photographs or financial data I may have lost. Patience with not knowing. So much not knowing, that it has become the very basis of life.

There is grace in a friend's phone call, a niece-in-law's old-fashioned letter in the mail, in familiar faces in Hollywood Squares boxes on a computer screen, in a poem well-written and well-read, in an astrological chart that portrays celestial forces aligning with all the chaos and news alerts and unfamiliarity of the formerly familiar.

There is grace in letting go, in just sitting and following the breath. That is enough.

Prompt: During shelter-in-place, have you discovered what works for you as an instrument of grace?

Disaster Soup

Denial CAN be a legitimate survival strategy, I often say, only half joking. It's one my family employed after my mother died at age 34. You'd have thought she had never existed. We never spoke of her—no stories, no memories. My grandmother, whose favorite saying was "What doesn't kill you makes you stronger," came over and cleaned out her things from the closet. Her shoes, her jeans, her shorts, her tops, her dresses. Gramma asked me if I wanted any of the dresses, most of which my mother had made herself. I was 14. They weren't my style, nor my size. Besides, having her clothes would break the denial spell. *No, no I don't.*

The denial spell worked for another 16 years or so, around the time of my first Saturn return, when I noticed I was numb. I felt no pain, the whiskey and cocaine made double-sure of that, but I felt no joy either. One day it dawned on me that maybe I should talk to the psychologist I kept convincing my public defender clients to see. Decades of grief work ensued, the legacy of denial.

Denial doesn't work for me now. There's no denying that white cop's knee on that black man's neck for 8 minutes and 46 seconds. There's no denying last year's disastrous crop failures back on my family's farms due to floods all spring and summer, making it too late to get crops in the ground and if by some miracle they were sown, they didn't ripen before the early freeze. Even all those farmers said—*I've never seen anything like it, not in my 60 years of farming.*

There's no denying the increased ferocity and frequency of the hurricanes, tornadoes, super cells, derechos, and summer heat waves. Of humidity so low that a loose chain on a travel trailer tow bar hitting the pavement can set off a raging wild fire.

There's no denying our government institutions have been gutted. Our constitution has been overridden. Our courts have been packed with judges who await the rapture, and a 4-year-old is in charge of the country.

And there's no denying that every time I set foot outside my door, I risk death, or serious illness, at least.

Denial just makes it last longer. The grief, the extinction of species, the decline of democracy, the quarantine. That much I've learned. Face it. Look at it. Feel it. Sob until you clutch your gut and collapse on the floor in a heap and you think you are going to die right there. Get up. Look around with your now clear eyes. March, write, sing, meditate, make your Disaster Soup.

Life goes on until it doesn't. You can't deny that, either.

Prompt: Denial.

What energizes you?

It sounds crazy at first, but reading energizes me. Sounds crazy because ostensibly, reading is a passive activity. For me, at least. I'm not one of those people who reads while on the treadmill or exercise bike. For me, it involves, ideally, a comfy chair and a cup of tea. And yet, while a general observer would say it looks like nothing much is going on, quite the opposite is true.

When reading about a harrowing trek along an icy mountain trail, my heart is racing. I'm huffing and puffing like I'm out there myself, all my attention on each carefully placed step that keeps me from plummeting down a steep abyss.

But more than that, reading about the England of Will Shakespeare, the Russia of Tolstoy, the China of Pearl Buck, the Middle Earth of Tolkien while sprawled on the couch in a bleak Midwestern farmhouse, gave me the energy to get myself to college, when that was a far from pre-ordained destination, and later to explore the world firsthand. Reading *Little Women* infused me with the energy to write my own stories. Reading books about personal transformation by Bay Area authors and teachers energized me to move across the country to study with them and change careers.

The moral of the story is—if you have young children in your life, teach them to love books and never underestimate the power of a well-crafted story to energize and change a life.

Patricia Morris

Patricia Morris is a Midwestern farm girl who grew up to be a trial lawyer. Then one day, after realizing she wasn't even a contentious person, she ran away to San Francisco to study Organization Development and Transformation at the California Institute of Integral Studies. After an 18-year career as a leadership consultant and coach in the medical field, she is exploring life beyond the workaday world.

Patricia dates her love of stories and good writing to sitting at the knee of her great aunt who was a children's librarian. Patricia made up stories to tell the cattle in the barnyard, made up imaginary playmates on the side of the schoolyard under the trees, and made up her life. She taught poetry writing at a senior citizen's day care program and has written for Rand McNally's *Vacation America, the Ultimate Road Atlas*.

Patricia loves living in Petaluma, California, where she again finds herself in the company of cows.

First Aid

Dad, I'm 55.
Just sit down, he said, kneeling in front of me on doorknob
knees.
And then with a gentleness that caught me by surprise,
he dabbed at my knee with a moistened cotton ball,
removing dirt and blood from the scrape,
taking great care not to pull too hard on its rawness.
This may sting, he said, spritzing the wound with Bactine.
But it was his tenderness that made me suck my breath in,
my eyes water.
His hands, artist's hands, square and sturdy
strong hands, shaking slightly now,
the hands of an old man.
He skillfully opened the band-aid
and laid it delicately across my knee.
There, he said, unbending stiffly,
patting me on the shoulder,
Good as new.

Prompt: Write about something that caught you by surprise.

Midnight at the dough-asis

Sleep Desert
I am prostrate on the bed
a yeasty doughball
bloated and sticky
like the Pillsbury Doughboy
trapped in Hell's proofing oven.
Beside me, the cat
miserable in her fur pajamas
is hogging the fan
sucking all the cool air
into her forbidden belly fluff.
A mosquito buzzes and lands on my face
but my flipper is too doughy
to swat it away.
I wonder idly if I taste like
a fresh baked biscuit.
The mosquito takes a sip
then buzzes over to the unbaked
baguette of my arm to drink again.
Lucky bug, this bakery will be open all night.

Prompt: I wonder.

Rioting and Violence on the Streets of the Emerald City

Yesterday
Security was easy.
Front doors went unlocked.
Bicycles, laid down
could sleep on the front lawn
all night, waking up when
the sprinklers started in the morning.
Today, I watch a squirrel
stealing sunflower chips from the bird feeder
and I am uneasy.
Tucked inside the house
with the fire on
hot tea and a scone
my feet are icy in wool socks.
A serpent of fear slithers down my spine.
I am terrified to lose my place;
that my house, my home, might become
a stranger.
The world outside is changing so fast
like a tornado tearing everything into tiny pieces
confetti in a hurricane.
I feel like Dorothy in her airborne house
hurling through a storm
having no idea what bizarre new world
we're about to fall into.
Waiting.

Waiting like my neighbors are waiting.
We are all waiting.
We sit huddled in our houses like rats
gnawing at each other and climbing the walls
communicating with outsiders
using window-blind Morse code.
Waiting,
the way a lame horse waits for the rancher
to bring his gun.
Like dinosaurs gazing up into ash-filled skies,
we are waiting to feel safe again.

Prompt: Write a blues poem. A blues poem typically takes on themes such as struggle, despair, bad weather, any suffering.

What energizes me?

Writing: becoming the river instead of drifting in the current
Creating: bringing something original into the world
a robust cup of coffee with cream swirled in—
the first sip that tingles like the elixir of life
laughing and making someone else laugh
a colorful yarn spun by a master weaver
giving the perfect unexpected gift
nature, in all its amazing forms
making & wearing silly hats
being on or in the water
spontaneous silliness
rocks and crystals
thunderstorms
Halloween
flirtations
exploring
collages
feeling
good
tea
U

Su Shafer

Su Shafer was creating stories and poems before she could pick up a pencil. She draws as naturally as she writes and her doodles are often sketches of a larger story unfolding internally. All matter matters and characters exist in every object, be it rock, mushroom, moth, or tea kettle—any and all are colorful characters in her world.

She resides in the Pacific Northwest, in a little Baba Yaga house near the entrance to The Hidden Wood. At night the trees dance and the frogs sing write-write, write-write.

Hello, Goodbye, and All That

Say goodbye to another victim of COVID-19: The Handshake. The longer we live with physical distancing, the harder it becomes to imagine a future where humans make skin-to-skin contact in public. Even though it's not official, I am mourning the passing of that old-fashioned gauge of confidence and character. How precious were those moments when we joined hands, creating bridges between us.

If the handshake as we knew it is dead, what will replace it? I hope it won't be some cheap approximation, like the virtual hug. I hate standing six feet away from loved ones with my arms curved at shoulder height holding nothing but air.

People are terrified of getting too close, which probably means the death of the friendly embrace, an even greater loss. But just as depressing would be a future with no crowds, so no noisy restaurants either, hence no need to tilt my better ear toward my companions, inviting their mouths closer. How sad to think of a world where the tickle of a secret on someone's breath is in danger of disappearing forever.

I personally won't be mourning the end of the high-five. That was one celebratory gesture I never managed without feeling like I was jarring something loose. But I will miss seeing that exuberant palm slap pass between others, especially if it's replaced with an elbow bump. The world is awkward enough without driving our bony parts toward each other. I'm not really troubled about the elbow bump catching on, though; it's too close range. And a physically distanced high-five could so easily be misinterpreted as, "Back off!" I am, however, more than a little nervous about namaste.

On the surface, a prayerful little bow seems like a good idea, but outside of yoga or meditation classes and ethnic groups which I, as an aging white lady, so don't belong to, namastes often smack of self-consciousness or condescension. How can you acknowledge another spirit as shining and tattered as your own without looking smug about it? I feel pretty much the same about placing my hand over my heart and bowing ever so slightly, like they do in the Middle East. Despite COVID-19's power to bring us to our knees, Americans seem ill-suited to any greeting that involves trying to look humble.

If you're like me, you've been trying to find a safe way to acknowledge a friend or acquaintance. I've thought about smiling and holding my upturned palms toward those I meet as if to say, "There you are! How delightful!" But now that we're all masked, this gesture is probably going to read more like, "OMG. What the f**k?"

Whenever I've considered trying to revive the peace sign, I think about my cynical youth, when flashing a Vee often meant, "I don't think you're cool, but let's just pretend I respect you."

Right now, I'm in the mood for something assertive, like tapping my right fist against my left clavicle in a salute that is probably a direct steal from some mercenary army or maybe a race of aliens on *Star Trek*. It would require practice and nuance to perfect. Thump that fist too hard or hold the pose too long and someone might think I am fomenting revolution. On some days, maybe I am, but most of the time, I just want a gesture that says, "I'm here, I'm alive, and I see you are, too."

Prompt: Saying Goodbye.

Behind The Mask

The term "Resting Bitch Face" had not been invented when I was in junior high school. In 1967, the idea that a woman would let her facial expression go unheeded, even for a moment, allowing herself to appear irritated or bored, was unthinkable. One could argue that this is still the case.

In the summer between seventh and eighth grade, my unfailingly cheerful mother told me that before she and my father married, she trained herself to sleep with her mouth closed so she would never snore. I had recently noticed my tendency to drool when I dozed off. Suddenly, I saw this unladylike habit as a future handicap. Feigning nonchalance, I asked her how she maintained control of her jaw while unconscious.

"Oh," she said with a shrug, "I just told myself to stop." She went on to tell me how, as a newlywed, she was so eager to be a good wife, she ironed my father's underwear. It was another chilling blow. Then, as now, I could barely manage to iron even a handkerchief. If being a successful woman required mastering my unconscious mind as well as the mysteries of the steam iron, I was doomed. There had to be something I could control.

I had already gotten pretty good at hiding frustration or displeasure from my father, who mocked me if I exhibited what he and my mother called pouting. How strange to learn later that pouty lips were considered attractive, sexy even, and that many women, at least in the movies, had men falling all over themselves trying to turn those frowns upside down. Stranger still, I had also noticed that in the movies, a woman who was hard to please always got her comeuppance in the end. Some humiliation or other was required before she could live happily ever after. And happily ever after meant choosing her man's pleasure over her own.

How much wiser to face the future wearing a mask of compliance, not that it was easy to mold one. I thought I was a fairly agreeable child, but I still remember the effort it took to curve the corners of my mouth in a Mona Lisa smile, how fervently I hoped it would make me appear enigmatic, interested, and interesting. I decided tilting my head slightly conveyed rapt attention, as if what others were saying was more important than what they were thinking about me. I even learned to kindle what felt like warmth in my eyes by widening them slightly at their outer corners. By the time I was in high school, my mask was in place. I didn't have to think about it anymore.

Thus the problem of Resting Bitch Face for me was circumvented long ago, although the line between looking eager to please and actually feeling that way has always been hard to draw. My biggest challenge these days is making sure I'm not automatically looking pleasant in unpleasant situations. I was probably smiling the night I was carjacked at gunpoint when I was eighteen. I can only hope that was one reason the gunman finally let me and my date out of the car: I must have looked more than a little crazy.

Prompt: What prepared you to be an adult?

Things to do on Your Deathbed

Don't let your life flash before your eyes. Look instead at the yellow plastic cup on your bedside table, the one with the bent straw tilted over its rim. Remember how good that last taste of water felt in your mouth, even though it was warm and stale.

There is a slight breeze in the room. Can you feel it floating across your forehead like a caress? Amplify that soft breath of air until you can remember a ride in a convertible, kite-flying on a beach, the stir of a lover moving close enough to kiss you.

If someone is holding your hand, squeeze it lightly. Feel the pressure of skin on skin and be grateful for all the places you've been touched, all the earth your feet have walked.

Let your memory bring you a smell, even if it's sauerkraut or limburger cheese: Trust your nose. You can follow it wherever you need to go.

Take a little trip around your body, all the soft and bony parts loosening their hold on your attention. They are not quite ready to leave you. Thank them for that.

Listen for your favorite sound: Crickets, morning birdsong, the rush of wind or rain. Once you hear it clearly, wait a little longer.

Now you can begin spinning the reel of memory back, back, and farther back until you arrive at the place you started. Take your last breath there.

There.

Prompt: What to do (modeled after "Things to Do in the Belly of the Whale" by Dan Albergotti).

What energizes you?

Before the pandemic, any trip or adventure involving a change of scene used to energize me. Even driving twenty freeway miles to Santa Rosa gave me a chance to remember that the world is wide and people are three-dimensional.

Last summer, after weeks of going nowhere, I had to start looking closer to home for the stimulation that fuels my creativity. This got me changing the scene around my house, which worked for a couple of months. Sorting, fixing, and rearranging can be its own kind of adventure, and often involves taking trips to the past, which is where most of my stories live. I enjoyed that burst of domesticity until repetition transformed pleasure into drudgery.

These days, so much of the larger world feels beyond my grasp. There's no place to go but in. With no adventures to energize me, I'm turning to language for inspiration. I love the long "o" sound in "lonely" and "remote," the way "regret" opens the door to graceful melancholy, how certain arrangements of syllables make a kind of music filled with the chimes of longing. I'm remembering that for writers, every word has its own physicality and energy, the way paint does for painters.

Some of a word's power comes from accumulated associations. If you're like me, the mention of "moon" triggers a glimmer of celestial light. "Frost" carries with it the temperature of ice. For me, the word "superb" flashes red, like a ripe apple, and "whisper" brings the sound of green leaves waving from summer's branches. These associations, some of them unique to me, help me see that if I'm paying attention to language, my isolation can be a ladder to climb, not just a dark well to fall into.

Words are a mobilizing force that takes me places and connects me to the past. They are what make me a writer.

Susan Bono

Susan Bono, a California-born teacher, freelance editor, and short-form memoirist, has facilitated writing workshops since 1993, helping hundreds of writers find and develop their voices. Her own work has appeared online, on stage, in anthologies, newspapers, and on the radio.

From 1995-2015, she edited and published a small press magazine called *Tiny Lights: A Journal of Personal Narrative*, as well as the online component that included quarterly postings of micro essays and a monthly forum dedicated to craft and process.

She was on the board of the Mendocino Coast Writers' Conference for more than a decade and was editor-in-chief of their journal, the *Noyo River Review*, for eight years.

Susan often writes about domestic life set in her small town of Petaluma.

She is the author of *What Have We Here: Essays about Keeping House and Finding Home*. Find out more at susanbono.com.

Whittling Dreams

Busy hands. Never-still hands. These days, hands are tapping, scrolling, swiping, typing. All day and well into the night. Fingers flying, two-handed texting using only thumbs. How do they do that? The posture is everywhere. Heads bent toward screens, bowing to the blue light. Have a spare minute? Go for that hit of dopamine! Another and another and another. Ping. Ring. Ding. News! The latest! Jokes, memes, ads, reminders, pleas for donations. Scroll through them all, don't skip a thing.

The next time you mask up and head out, stop for a minute and look up from your device. Everywhere eyes are focused on little machines. Few people remain still, just being, watching, contemplating. The circumferences of their personal spaces are small, no gazing outward at a beautiful autumn day, letting the mind wander, taking in the fresh breezes (in better, non-smoky days here on the West Coast). No relaxing into expansion towards the horizon, letting the eyes drift where they may, alighting on a fanciful cloud shape, the peak of a mountain, or just the other side of the street. You will see them indoors and out. Standing in line at the post office, head in the familiar tilt, elbows out, ever the downward gaze. Instant stimulation, not a moment left to chance. Boredom cut off at the pass. Get those fingers busy. Keep the hands in motion.

Nothing really concrete to show for all this digital activity at day's end. No little houses made to set on shelves, no vegetables lovingly reaped from the garden, not even baseball mitts being slapped with a fist. Another day conducting life online. Zoom meetings, iChats, FaceTimes, emails, and texts. Busy hands indeed. But not so productive, at least not tangibly. One is left with a jangle in the brain along with carpal tunnel syndrome. Our worlds shrink in real time as they enlarge exponentially into the cyberworld. The here and now suffers. The concept of being in the moment is co-opted by frantic fingers wanting more, more, more.

How soothing to think of sitting quietly in the soft light, whittling a piece of wood, letting the mind roam, the eyes wander. And to end up with an item one has created. A little house on a shelf, different from all the others. Unique, with a personality of its own. Not ordered online and delivered by a harried driver trying to evade COVID.

Prompt: Hands.

Fishing with Dad

I am casting about for warm memories of safety in my youth, but perhaps I have stuffed my brain with stories and more stories of how unsafe I felt. On guard, walking on eggshells to avoid my mother's wrath which might erupt at any moment. Is that really true? Surely there were times of joy and security and feeling safe at home. Maybe fishing with my father at Indian Lake the summer we rented a cottage because our kitchen was being renovated. A whole summer by the lake.

After work, my Dad would drive out to the cottage to join us. He would retrieve his tackle box from the back porch and load it into the boat. Was it a rowboat? Or a little craft with a small engine? Probably the latter. He would bait the hook for me, and I would throw out a line per his instructions as he steered. It didn't take long before I felt a tug on the line. He talked me through reeling in my catch, keeping steady, and allowing no slack. Eventually I pulled in an ugly, scary-looking fish. A bullhead, Dad called it. Its most remarkable feature was the array of stingers jutting out from the sides of its flat head. They were capable of causing a lot of pain. Dad helped me. He didn't want me to get zapped, so he worked my catch off the hook gingerly and threw it back into the lake. And then we did it all over again.

I loved having my father all to myself, and I felt special that he would carve out time for me—a girl—to take on this adventure. My brother, older by three years, would have been the more likely candidate. Maybe he was off with a friend or at Little League practice. So, it was just Dad and me in that boat. I reveled in being the chosen one, the only offspring invited along. I felt cared for in his handling of the threatening fish. He didn't want me to get hurt.

In retrospect, I see his protection made me feel warm and fuzzy. Yes. Daddy wanted to keep me safe. But it occurs to me now that also it kept me feeling afraid and incompetent. Poor Dad! Doing his best to create a bonding experience. But I think I might have grown by being taught how to tackle that thorny, slimy, zinging creature, how to get it off the line and back into the lake without putting myself in harm's way. I was left feeling I needed a protector, that I couldn't keep myself safe. I think I may have been nine, old enough to learn to deal with dicey situations. Perhaps I would have been better served by trying it myself. I would not have been left feeling disempowered and incapable, looking for a savior.

Prompt: Write about a place where you felt safe.

COVID Rant

September 2020

When I woke up this morning, the heaviness had not lifted. The despair, the ennui filled the room and kept me pressed to the bed. I didn't want to move. Greet the day? What for? Nothing matters. Nothing is appealing. What is the point? Oh, to muster the energy to slog through the atmosphere thick with negativity and dismissiveness. I am tired. I am sick of it all.

Awakening again to the voices of the construction workers just outside my window. Will they be banging, sawing, pounding, yelling, or hammering today? They have been at this since last December and it continues. I am tired of them, the noise of the garbage trucks, yesterday's heat inside which did not dissipate even with windows open to the nighttime coolness.

I am tired of Covid. I don't want to wear a mask and be careful. And I am angry at others who don't and aren't. As if that weren't enough, there are the frightening erratic wildfires and the color-coded Air Quality Index warnings, Yellow, Orange, Red and Purple. Masking up to avoid smoke as well as Covid. I am tired of checking AQI multiple times a day. A month ago I was unfamiliar with the term air quality index. It has become an obsession.

I am tired of figuring out what to eat. And what not to eat. And of making myself take a walk when I don't want to. I am tired of social distancing. I am tired of the phrase itself and all it entails. I want to hug my daughters and frolic with my grandchildren. I want to prepare a lovely meal for my friends and invite them into my home. I want to be social without distancing or Zooming. I want to get back to normal, although it is becoming more apparent every day that there is no such thing. The world as we knew it is forever changed. Learning to embrace this liminal space is our only hope of finding any semblance of equanimity. And I am tired.

Prompt: I don't want to . . .

What energizes you?

As I sign into Zoom for a writing group, I find I am looking forward to gathering with fellow writers, but I wouldn't say I feel particularly energized by doing so. That comes later. After we greet one another and catch up a little, our leader offers the first prompt. I sit in the in-between-time, not having let the events of the day fade all the way into the background just yet, not quite able to transition into the spirit of the moment. I have no idea what to write about and the prompt may not feel particularly interesting or relevant. My mind wanders, the resistance begins to build. I fidget. I need a drink of water. I want a snack. I really should make that phone call, write that email, start a load of laundry.

Then I remember. Just put pen to page. Just start. Write anything. Anything at all. Write, "I don't know what to write." Write it again. And maybe again. Write, "This is a boring prompt. I don't want to think about this tonight. I am tired of this topic. Surely, these Zoom participants are tired of me. I am too boring to exist. No one will care. I don't care."

Get it down. Keep the hand moving. And then, invariably, the energy starts to build, the pen takes on a life of its own and just keeps scribbling down the words that begin to pour out. The words that boring prompt has excavated. Not all the words. Sometimes in my rush to get it down I can't produce exactly the phrase I know I want, so I just draw a line and keep going, letting it flow, trying to write as fast as the words are appearing, trying to keep up. Knowing I can go back later and fill in the blanks when my brain has finally had time to catch up. The energy builds, and I can feel it. And suddenly I am aware I am in the zone. I am taken to a place I had no idea I would visit. On a really good night I might even describe it as a fire in the belly. This is not to say that the finished piece is necessarily highly regarded by me or by anyone else, but the process becomes pure energy. Exhilaration sets in. I am getting it down. I am getting it out. I am finding my voice.

This hit of adrenaline sustains me. This connection with my unconscious is addictive, even though I don't often push myself to sit down and write on my own. Usually I let life's distractions take over and keep me from facing the empty page. It is easy to run away. But in a writing group I have company. I have made a commitment. And there are ears which will hear my words as I read them aloud. There are people who will listen to me. This too is pure energy, taking the risk of reading whatever I produced from my gut, letting others see who I really am and how I really think. This is stepping out of the box. This is what energizes me. This is what keeps me coming back for more.

Susie Moses

Susie Moses is inspired by prompts provided by teachers of creative writing groups she is drawn to attend. She is astonished to sit back and observe her pen take off in directions she had not anticipated and to watch her brain latch on to thoughts she was unaware of having. She hopes someday to evolve to writing from her own prompts, but for now she embraces generative classes as steps on her path to writing independently.

Susie has been published in *The Write Spot: Writing as a Path to Healing*, available at Amazon.

My Perfect Family

In 1955, when I was seven, I was aware my family was different from the other families who lived in the new subdivision in Santa Clara, California. For one thing my father was a merchant seaman, gone for months at a time, shipping out of San Francisco to the Orient. He brought back unusual toys: A slender doll dressed in a kimono nestled in a wooden box. Six different ornate wigs, each in their own little box, lined both sides of the doll's compartment; a pink and yellow plastic toy that opened like a small umbrella. At the touch of a switch on the handle, pink and yellow plastic flower petals fanned out and twirled like a miniature carnival ride.

I showed these to my friends in the neighborhood, but I wouldn't let them play with these treasures. Instead, we decorated our bicycle handlebars with cherry blossoms. Using clothespins, we attached playing cards on the frames of our bikes so the cards made a loud clicking noise when they fluttered through the spokes of the wheels. Triumphant, we paraded up and down the sidewalks.

My father brought us "go-aheads," a flip-flop type of footwear called "geta" in Japanese, similar to flip-flops, but with a flat wooden base and three little pieces of wood on the bottom, elevating our feet off the ground. A thick corded fabric attached from the top of the sandal to the back of the sandal, keeping them on our feet. I dressed as a Japanese lady for a school Halloween party wearing the go-aheads and a kimono that my father also brought from Japan. My mother rolled my long hair around a small towel and pinned everything on top of my head, resembling a pompadour. I won second place in the costume contest. My father never saw me in that costume, or any other costume.

He was not a daddy that came home at dinnertime. There were no Sunday drives. He wasn't around for school days or school plays. He wasn't there for birthday parties with aunts, uncles, and cousins. I remember only one holiday with him.

It was Christmas Eve. My inebriated father was behind the wheel of our '57 Chevy. While the rest of the world was celebrating the coming of Our Savior, I was in the backseat of our car, hugging my knees and trying not to cry. I looked out the window through the rainy drizzle and saw smeared traffic lights. Red and green lights that should have been happy Christmas colors. In the front seat, my mother begged my father to let her drive.

I pretended I had a perfect family. That's what I told my friend who lived across the street in Santa Clara. Sitting in her front yard, next to the strong-smelling white alyssum, I said, "I have a perfect family, a mother, a father, and two girls."

I knew I was lying, but I didn't care. Maybe I thought that if I said it often enough, it would come true.

I wanted to believe it so much that I was willing to lie about it, committing the ultimate sin my mother would punish me for if she knew about it.

For many years after, whenever I smelled alyssum I was filled with feelings of guilt about my lie. It was as if the smell mocked me, wanting to punish me over and over for lying.

What I didn't tell my playmate was that my father was often drunk and angry. He would lash out at whoever irritated him. One time, he kicked our dog out the patio door. I watched the little black dog sail through the air and land on a pile of dirt. My heart broke and made me afraid of making my father angry.

I invited friends over when my father was away at sea. Mostly, we played games outside, jumping rope, one foot off the gutter, red rover, tag, statues, and roller skating.

I didn't go to friends' houses often, but I imagined them sitting down to family dinners together, sharing how their day went.

After a year in Santa Clara, my youngest sister was born and we moved in with my father's parents in a three-bedroom flat in the Mission District of San Francisco. My father drifted away to live a life in the Tenderloin. My grandfather passed away four years later.

I no longer pretended I had a perfect family.

But, where did I get the idea of what a perfect family is?

Television, of course. My favorite show in the fifties and sixties was the *Donna Reed Show*. Perky Donna Stone and her handsome although naïve, doctor-husband, with his office right in their home. I thought their son, Jeff, was dreamy and I related to the daughter, teenage Mary. *The Nelson Family* validated my belief of what the perfect family was: A doting mother and wife, a loving father and husband—with two well-behaved children.

Our family felt like a female version of the TV show *My Three Sons* with a grandmother, a mother, and three girls.

My perfect family.

Even though my perfect family did not include my imperfect father, and even though I felt shame whenever I thought about him, I cared about him. I was devastated when everything he brought back from the Orient was destroyed in a fire. When I was sixteen, he died. He was only thirty-seven. As a Marine Corps veteran he had a military funeral. At the cemetery, a soldier stood to the right of me and played Taps. That mournful sound filled the air on a calm afternoon. Another soldier handed my mother the carefully folded flag that had been draped over my father's coffin. She later gave the triangular-folded flag to me. The pain I felt whenever I looked at it never subsided so I gave the flag away. I wish I would have kept it. Instead, I honor my father in my heart, knowing he did the best he could.

Prompt: "You don't grow up missing what you never had, but throughout life there is hovering over you an inescapable longing for something you never had."—Susan Sontag

Christmas Letter, December 2020

Dear Special Person,

I love sending and receiving Christmas cards, especially the sparkly ones. I hope I receive a card from you this year. Meanwhile, here's an idea of how the year 2020 went for me and Jim.

I wonder, is there a silver lining to the debacle of 2020?

I feel as though my brain went on vacation and left my body home. I don't know exactly when that happened. Hmmm... a look through my diary might provide a clue.

March 19
Oven stopped working. No explanation. Worked one day, then poof!

March 20
Bought a gas range. My last excursion before "shelter in place." Jim became our designated shopper.

April 3
Installers left new stove in middle of kitchen floor. They took the old stove and drove away. We discovered oven door was damaged, making oven unusable.

April 11
Installers picked up damaged range and delivered another range. We didn't let them leave until we inspected it. There was damage on the back, but it was cosmetic, so we let them go. Then we noticed a gas leak whenever we turned on the

oven. But we didn't call to get it fixed because, you know, possible COVID-19 exposure.

April 18
I hold my breath every time I turn the oven on, waiting for an explosion. But I'm still too worried to let anyone in the house. Like so many things, I'm dealing with this dilemma by not dealing with it.

May 10, Mothers' Day
We have our first of many family Zoom parties. The "kids" surprised me with a virtual experience on the Disneyland Jungle Cruise ride. Our son, Rob, and his daughter, Vivien, wrote the humorous script. Rob narrated. I loved it.

Memorial Day Weekend
We take a chance on sharing possible COVID-19 exposure and have our annual Memorial Weekend party, celebrating Rob's birthday and relaxing in our piazza. We miss family and friends who usually join us. Are you wondering why we call our outdoor area a "piazza" instead of a patio? We were inspired after our 2015 cruise to the Mediterranean to transform our outdoor area into the type of cobblestoned courtyards found in Italy. We sit in our piazza and remember when we could travel.

July 24—September 27
The sixth book in the Write Spot series is published. This is the book I've been aiming for, the one I dreamed about since 2003. *The Write Spot: Writing as a Path to Healing* is better than I imagined it. I host 15 Zoom events to share excerpts and promote the anthology.

July 27

Began work on the next Write Spot anthology.

Also began editing a friend's novel. Alla is Russian, grew up in Harbin, China in the 1930s, when Harbin was occupied by the Japanese (which is where and when her novel takes place).

August 1

My body is turning into the shape of a question mark from too many hours at the computer day after day after day. My future as a hunched over old lady flashes like a neon sign. I hobble along, pursuing my passion of working with writers at Jumpstart Writing Workshops and Writers Forum (all on Zoom).

September 10

I'm getting annoyed with my loss of memory. I can't seem to hold onto thoughts. During an evening bath, I'll think about the anti-itch lotion I need to apply. By the time I'm in bed, I realize I forgot about the medicine. I resend emails, not recalling what I sent the day before. I don't even know what I'm forgetting. I'm beginning to think it doesn't matter. I'm wondering what does matter.

September 12

What matters is being kind to people.

October 1

I felt adventurous and made some appointments: Facial, manicure, haircut. Then I got nervous and cancelled all appointments. I figured everyone's hair is looking a little ragged and no one can see the hairs on my chin under my mask.

I feel like I'm walking underwater wearing lead weights for shoes.

October 8
I was exposed to someone who tested positive for COVID-19. I self-quarantined for 14 days. I thought that would be easy because I like being home and my writing business is pretty much a one-person activity. It was harder than I thought it would be. Maybe it was the psychological aspect of having to be confined, rather than a choice to stay home. I don't like shopping, but I wanted to see and feel the merchandise. I don't miss going out, but I do like the option of going out freely, with no worries.

Life is feeling like a slog.

October 28
I start attending a Zoom Qi Gong class.

November 14
The gas smell has mysteriously disappeared. Lesson learned: I can let some things go. I don't have to be responsible to fix everything.

November 21
Jim and I test negative for COVID-19. A time when a negative is a positive!

December 8
I start attending a Zoom class called "An Exercise to Restore Your Body's Magic with Judith" and add a Feldenkrais class because I got a discount from signing up for Judith's class.

December 9
I added Zoom yoga nidra to my self-care activities. I look forward to this deep relaxation.

December 11 Afternoon

There are six things I could/should do: Practice Qi Gong, practice the exercises to restore my body's magic, practice Feldenkrais, attend a meditation group a friend invited me to, work on the next Write Spot anthology, or listen to my yoga nidra recording.

I decide to eat popcorn, enjoy a drink, and read a book.

In signing up for all these classes, I wonder what I'm searching for. What am I longing for? Is there something broken that needs to be fixed? Is anxiety and uncertainty the new normal? Am I searching for something that is elusive?

December 15

I'm currently reading four books (not unusual for me). Not one of them holds my interest.

I brought in six boxes of holiday decorations from storage. I opened the boxes and pulled out snow globes, figurines, little village scenes, ornaments for a garland, and ornaments for the tree. I took a break and checked my email. A message prompted me to search for a book to suggest for my book club, which led to rearranging book shelves. I thought about dinner. I decided to look up recipes to fix something new for dinner. Surveying the stacks of books and ornaments covering every horizontal surface in the parlor, and recipes covering the kitchen table, I ordered take-out food.

December 18

Alla's book has been published, which is a marvelous reward for her hard work.

I'm still working on the next Write Spot anthology, fingers crossed (making it really hard to type) that it will be published Spring 2021.

December 20

I have lost words. Too often, the word I'm looking for isn't even on the tip of my tongue, let alone in my head somewhere. I wonder if this is part of being overwhelmed or is it a by-product of aging? I can't even muster the energy to freak out. I feel like I'm living in the twilight zone.

Maybe my brain went on vacation in Harbin, China, or left the house with the damaged stove, or maybe I was affected by the gas leak.

Or maybe I got so overwhelmed with rules and remembering to bring a mask when going outside and wondering if I should even be going out . . . maybe I'm on overload.

December 21

The solstice has me thinking. There has to be a silver lining to 2020! There has to be something good that came from this year. The first thing that comes to mind is that a dear friend and her husband had a beautiful baby girl, a reminder that life goes on.

The next beautiful thing is the variety of activities available through Zoom, connecting with friends, making new friends, learning new things.

I appreciate the quiet and calm with fewer cars driving on our normally busy street.

Stores are less crowded. People seem to be smiling behind their masks, at least their eyes are smiling. Everyone is mostly polite and considerate. I send love and compassion to those who are angry, understanding they are having a harder time or are less fortunate than I am.

I am grateful for ample food, a cozy house, family, friends, and plenty to do.

What I have learned in this crazy year is that connections, keeping friends and loved ones close, is more important now than ever.

Sisters Diane and Nancy said I could share their holiday letter with you.

Hugs, Marlene

Nancy and Diane's 2020 Holiday Newsletter

Happy Holidays!

We didn't go anywhere.

We didn't do anything.

Happy New Year!

Love from Nancy and Diane

Prompt: How was your year?

Things I Never Thought I Would Do

How my life changed after the March 15, 2020 shelter in place order.

I never thought I would hand over grocery shopping duties to my husband. Since I'm the preparer of meals, I have been the one grocery shopping since we were married in 1969. We decided only one of us should go out in public, risking possible COVID-19 exposure. What a change to have someone else to bring home the bacon and many other items I didn't know we liked or needed: capers, Boursin cheese, candied pecans, tuna in a pouch (not recommended), kosher dill pickles (confirmed: we don't like them).

I never thought I would eat food past its expiration date. Okay, expired by only a few days. Maybe a month in one or two instances of packaged goods. At this point, expiration dates are just suggestions. In the early days of shelter in place, my husband thought we should stock up on staples, especially canned and packaged items. But we couldn't eat everything within the "best by" dates. I'm grateful for our bounty and aware that too many people are experiencing hunger, so I'm unwilling to waste food.

In September, I felt there were enough safety protocols in place to venture into grocery stores. By then, my absent-mindedness had grown to dementia-like proportions. I would buy ingredients for dinner, forgetting I already had plans and ingredients for a different dinner.

I'm tired of thinking about food. I don't want to plan meals. I'm tired of making decisions. Like Mary Poppins,

I want to nod my head and have nutritious and delicious meals appear on my table.

I just want easy and simple.

Thank goodness my computer has the date on it, otherwise I would not know what day it is. My calendar pages are blank. With no appointments scheduled, it's hard to tell one day apart from another.

I never thought I would wear a mask everywhere, especially into a bank! Adding to the stress of leaving the safety of home, there was the thought process before leaving home and carefully considering needs versus wants. I want that item but do I need it enough to warrant possible COVID-19 exposure? If the answer was yes, there were the mental gymnastics of choosing a comfortable mask. One that wouldn't fog up my glasses or slide down my nose. Having chosen a mask, I needed to remember to bring it when I left the house.

When will I stop thinking all excursions might result in COVID-19 exposure?

I also wonder when we'll stop putting mail and all deliveries in the garage, quarantining for 24 hours.

Never did I ever think I would shop for anything and everything online: gluten-free Stroopwafels, socks, supplements, liquid hand soap, indoor lights, outdoor lights, light bulbs, a desk calendar, moisturizer creams, a blow-up punching bag for granddaughter (maybe I should buy one for myself), recipe books, weight loss books, a foot massager.

I never thought I could facilitate writing workshops in real time on a computer. I'm technology-challenged. I can look at something, and it will break. At first, the thought of facilitating writing workshops online terrified me. I have been known to get the computer to strange places causing my husband to ask, "How did you do that?" I never know what keyboard buttons nor what clicks caused the never-seen-before (and never-seen-again) page to appear.

But I dove in and it worked. I interacted with people all over the world with the common goal of writing together.

At first, I wondered what is this thing, Zoom? It was a verb. Now it's a proper noun. Zoom is the new coffee shop/bar/living room gathering place. Meeting up on Zoom has become an almost daily activity, repeating the most used phrases of the year, "Can you hear me?" and "You're muted."

Get up at 6:30 am to attend a 7:30 am movement/dance class. Me? I never expected that. I learned about Diane Dupuis and her GROOVE moment, took the plunge, and joined her class. It was a miracle! With knee injuries, I thought I would never be able to dance again. Somehow, I was able to move with minor knee pain. I love Diane's spirit, admire her energy, and enjoy her bouncy personality. I danced with no worries. I was reminded of junior high Friday afternoon dances, minus the awkwardness of boys.

I never dreamed I would howl on my porch nightly at 8 pm. Then listen, hearing neighbors also howling. This was to show support to medical personnel. I had another reason for making noise. I wanted my voice to be heard. And I wanted to hear my neighbors' voices. I wanted to feel connected.

The idea of attending porch concerts by musicians who live a block up our lane never crossed my radar. Thursdays, Hannah and Ben stood on their balcony and serenaded us. Two doors down, on Sunday afternoons, Steve on keyboard and Robbie on saxophone entertained neighbors relaxing in lawn chairs up and down the sidewalk. We felt like we were at dinner theatre, minus the noise of crockery and glassware. We were amazed at how no one talked during the performance, respectful of the musicians nurturing us in difficult times.

I never would have believed I'd watch *PBS NewsHour* every night, until the repetition wore me down, and I had trouble getting to sleep. Then I watched Friday nights only. Soon after, I got my news fix from Facebook.

Instant gratification became more important than ever. I dusted dressers, tops of chair rails, shelves, knick-knacks. I vacuumed one end of the house to the other including lamp shades. I packed eight boxes for the thrift store, recycled reams of redundant papers and magazines. Went through all my clothes and memorabilia, kept most, but found some to pass on. Being surrounded by pleasant objects in a clean house helped lessen my anxiety and restored a sense of tranquility and serenity.

Fears and coping

A friend emailed, "I'm rattled right now, no question. Perhaps for good."

I was surprised because she is strong, stoic, and genius-smart, not a person easily rattled. I wanted to know more. I responded, "If we could visit in person, perhaps, we could talk about what is going on. But I wonder if we're talked out about certain subjects. We go round and round these days, saying the same things over and over. It feels like an endless cycle. I've been thinking how many of us live in fear right now. What I wonder is . . . how does that affect our health and what are the long-term ramifications of living in fear?"

I wish we could all be happy with no worries and no fears. Just content to be. Just for a moment. Or an hour. A day would be nice, too.

Comfort food took on a new meaning. It was more than comfort food. It was about how to cope with feeling scared. When food filled my belly, there was more than a feeling of satiation. There was a feeling of we're going to be okay. We can handle this. I tell myself this is just a moment in time. It's temporary. But I know we are forever changed.

Adding to my stress level was realizing my fears. I could contract COVID-19 and die, but first, I had better finish *The Write Spot: Writing as a Path to Healing.* I didn't want to disappoint the contributors. I felt a strong urge to say and do all that holds importance for me before there is no more me. Family was first on my list of people to make sure they knew I loved them and cared about them.

Part of my coping was to establish a routine and try to make each day meaningful. Rather than mindless mental meandering, I realized I needed to establish goals, also known as my to-do list, which was three pages long, typed, double-spaced.

Whittling down my to-do list worked until it didn't. Somewhere along the way I lost my ability to think, to focus, to make decisions. I just wanted to eat popcorn and watch reruns of *Jane, The Virgin* and *Monk* and *Rick Steve's* travel shows. I often thought about a line from Monk, "Spirits are easy to break, but not impossible to repair." I needed that kind of hope.

I needed to find a purpose. My writing work gave me a feeling of purpose—more than busy work—a feeling of accomplishment. But, as a writer friend noticed about her writing, she lost her mojo. So did I. I hoped it was just taking a rest and not completely gone.

Rather than chastise myself for what I wasn't getting done, I decided to appreciate what I was accomplishing, even if it was just making my bed, brushing my teeth, and crossing off one thing on my to-do list each day.

I know I'll rally and get back into a comfortable rhythm—maybe not today, but maybe tomorrow. Or the next day.

Perhaps my goal should be acceptance of myself and acceptance of the way things are right now. I don't have to like what is going on, but it's fruitless to struggle with changing what can't be changed. It is possible to change how I think about things. That is an ongoing challenge.

What is important

In September 2020, Northern California experienced extremely high temperatures and smoky days from wildfires. Checking the air quality became a daily activity. What was important was keeping cool—literally and figuratively—wearing a cooling cloth around my neck and staying hydrated. Early mornings, there was a feeling of the freshness of a new day not yet tainted with air too smoky to breathe and tensions too hot to handle.

As political fatigue replaced coronavirus fatigue, it became even more important to practice soothing techniques. Meditating and yoga helped access inner calm and offered assurance we will be okay.

What worked

Stepping outside and taking deep breaths was an immediate stress reducer.

I felt a sense of purpose as well as peacefulness while I watered outdoor plants and clipped off dead flowers.

It was important to keep a positive attitude and be hopeful. Watching John Krasinski's "Some Good News" on YouTube confirmed my faith in the goodness of people.

When I went out, I silently gave thanks to strangers, as we tilted our heads, reminding me of the "Howdy" salute, cowboys tipping their hats. I appreciated simple gestures of "we're in this together," as people stepped out of my path.

A new way of thinking about these surreal times helped: Changes, challenges, opportunities—all rolled together.

Gratitude

I'm grateful for the pleasant surprises that sheltering in place brought.

My uncle phoned to see how I'm doing. Those conversations led to deep reveals about his parents and his siblings. After he dies, I'll be the oldest living relative on that side of the family. I'm too young to be the oldest. Better than the alternative, though.

I joined two book clubs. One with my daughter and my ten-year-old granddaughter (my son's daughter). Over the summer and into autumn we read my granddaughter's choices: *The Wizard of Oz*, *Black Beauty*, *I Am Malala* (juvenile version), *Anne of Green Gables*, and *A Tree Grows in Brooklyn*. Our conversations led to deep and meaningful discussions about life, emotions, and people, bringing a closeness we would not have experienced in "normal" times.

The other book club with writers and people involved in writing communities helped to get me out of the hole I was feeling I was in. This book club became like the coffee klatches of the 1950s as we settled into our routine of Zooming from our homes, or a travel trailer in one case, chatting about books and life in general.

Although 2020 has been a challenge, it has also been an opportunity to practice new behavior. I'm noticing more, quietly observing, being patient, reaching out, and understanding in ways I had never before experienced.

I have been able to evaluate what is important, to recognize what isn't working, and to let go of negative thinking. Things that used to bother me no longer bother me. Without the distractions and activities of a "normal" year, 2020 has been an opportunity for reflection, resulting in growth and change.

This past year has taught me about grace.

I'm thankful for these unexpected gifts.

Prompt: Expect the unexpected.

What energizes you?

What energizes me is writing, working with writers, and dancing. I'm going to hand the baton over to Diane Dupuis, my amazing GROOVE facilitator/dance teacher who eloquently expresses the joy of GROOVE.

Diane:

Although I was unemployed on March 13th when shelter in place happened in Montreal—I was still in shock with the sudden halt that was put on different aspects of everyday life, and eventually just about every aspect of our lives.

For the first 6 days I sat and watched as things played out. My main direct loss was not being able to GROOVE 3 or 4 times a week. Moving my body, even though it can be achy and painful (thanks to fibromyalgia, arthritis, and menopause), is still the best way to keep me from getting even more stiff and sore. Those yummy post GROOVE endorphins were missed!

I am not one who loves to follow videos or dance on my own, but I knew if there were others, I would be up to dancing in a new format.

On Saturday March 21, my usual day of the week to give my GROOVE class, I decided to give GROOVE on Zoom a try.

Fear can be a great deterrent . . . I don't have the right space, I don't have enough bandwidth, I don't have a good enough computer, how weird will it be just dancing alone in my son's old room on camera?

But I did it anyway, and was blessed to have 28 people join me! They all missed dancing just as much as I did! Throwing fear aside—I decided to try it out for 7 days and I haven't stopped! In January 2021, we celebrated my 300th class on Zoom. We meet the same time every morning, an hour together dancing our hearts out in the safety of our own homes.

I am grateful for my GROOVERs for joining me. Some attend a couple of times a week, or just on the weekend. They do what they can when they can. Their love and support has been immeasurable.

My body at first was saying—WHAT THE HECK IS HAPPENING!!?? But I am kind and gentle to it and really don't stress it out too much outside our one hour of happy sing-along dancing.

I have danced through a kidney stone, herniated disk in my back and severe knee pain to name a few ailments.

I am so glad I faced my fears and started GROOVEing on Zoom. I know it has been essential for my mind, body and soul. Daily GROOVEing has given me purpose and so much JOY. I love connecting and getting to see my participants' smiling faces every day!!!

On the days that I attend Diane's Zoom GROOVE, I have more energy and definitely a positive outlook. Thank goodness for helpers like Diane.

Marlene Cullen

Marlene Cullen would like to say her stories are made of bone and gristle or mortar and bricks. She would like to think her writing is strong with solid foundations. But sometimes when she bites into them, she finds fluff, like that spun confection sold at carnivals. But if one of her stories sticks to you like cotton candy, well then, that's a good thing!

Writing Resources

Freewrites

Welcome to writing freely!

Welcome to a writing experience where the most important person is you.

Using the freewrite method of writing, you can learn to write quickly and effortlessly. Writing prompts will help ignite your writing. During this journey, you will make discoveries that can lead to transformational changes.

All you need is a notebook and a fast-moving pen or an electronic writing tablet, a timer, and a willingness to write. Uninterrupted time is beneficial to focus and concentrate.

There are a few guidelines to follow:

- Write freely.
- Write quickly.
- Don't pause to think.
- Don't cross out.
- Don't worry about spelling, punctuation, or grammar.
- Don't critique as you write.
- Follow the prompt . . . or not.

Choose a writing prompt

Start with a writing prompt from this book or a prompt on my blog, The Write Spot Blog.

Look around. Write about what you see: a particular item, writing on a book cover or on a piece of paper. A prompt can be a color, or something that catches your eye as you scan the area.

One of the easiest prompts to inspire writing is "I remember . . ."

Write whatever is on your mind. If the prompt is "trees" and your mind shifts to your first car, that's fine. Write about your first car. There is no wrong way to approach this writing practice. Whatever is on your mind is the best thing to be writing about.

Use a variety of prompts for your freewrites. The prompt can be fun and playful. The prompt might inspire memoir-type writing. Try new things. If you are a memoirist, write fiction every so often. If you mostly write fiction, try writing a true story. If you don't consider yourself a poet, try writing poetry. Experiment with different styles of writing.

The prompts are what you make of them. You can go light and stay on the surface, skate on the edge, or you can go deep and explore personal situations. You might discover solutions to problems.

Mechanics

Keep your hand moving across the page or your fingers dancing across the keyboard. Let yourself go. Lean into the experience of writing freely.

Don't over-think and don't try too hard. Let your imagination take over and write whatever comes up; the result might include surprising revelations. This type of writing is for your personal enjoyment, for self-discovery, and perhaps a spark for future writing.

Don't pause to think. There is tremendous energy in first thoughts. If we stop to think while we write, we can get lost in analyzing and second-guessing.

Don't cross out while you are writing in this free-association style. Don't worry about getting words or concepts exactly right. Be open to whatever flows out.

Don't worry about spelling, punctuation, or grammar. That's what the editing process is for.

Stretch, shrug, and breathe

Just as an athlete stretches to limber up before practice, you can do the same before writing.

Roll your shoulders in a forward circle a few times, then reverse the direction. Rotate your head in a circle, reverse direction. Stretch your arms and release the stretch. Roll your hands and wrists in circles.

Notice where there is tension. Release tension by breathing into it. Take some deep breaths in. Relax and let go on the outbreaths. Shed what might be holding you back from writing. Cast aside all "shoulds."

Leave your inner critic at the door. Shrug off the editor that sits on your shoulder. Do not judge your writing while you write.

Set timer for 15 or 20 minutes.

Read the prompt you have chosen. Start writing. Follow the prompt—or not. You are free to write whatever you want. It's more important that you pay attention to what's on your mind than the prompt.

Let go of your ideas about what perfect writing means. Give yourself permission to accept whatever comes up.

When stuck

If you can't think of what to write, simply repeat the prompt, or write: *What I really want to say* . . . and keep going. Follow your mind where it takes you. Just write.

Keep your pen moving or your fingers flying across your keyboard, even if you think you have nothing to say. Trust yourself. Trust the process. This is the place to feel free to practice writing. No one is going to read your work, unless you invite them to.

Neither judge nor be critical of your writing. This type of writing practice is for your own enjoyment and for exploring your path on this writing journey.

You can write the truth, fiction, or some of both.

You can learn more about freewrites in the previous Write Spot books and on The Write Spot website. www.TheWriteSpot.us

Recommended Books

A list of books that might help you on your writing journey. You can read how-to books on writing memoir. You can also read memoirs and use them as textbooks to learn how to write memoir.

Memoirs and Books on Writing Memoir

Alexie, Sherman—*You Don't Have to Say You Love Me*

Brautigan, Ianthe—*You Can't Catch Death*

Couvreux, Janis—*Sail Cowabunga!*

Fitzgerald Carter, Zoe—*Imperfect Endings*

Fu, Ping—*Bend, Not Break*

Karr, Mary—*The Art of Memoir* and *The Liar's Club*

Lefkowitz, Frances—*To Have Not*

Walls, Jeanette—*The Glass Castle*

Books on Writing

Cameron, Julia—*Walking in this World*

DeMarco-Barrett, Barbara—*Pen on Fire*

Frank, Thaisa—*Finding Your Writer's Voice: A Guide to Creative Fiction*

Hale, Constance—*Sin and Syntax*

Hugo, Richard—*The Triggering Town: Lectures and Essays on Poetry and Writing*

Leonard, Linda Schierse—*The Call to Create*

Lloyd, Carol—*Creating A Life Worth Living*

Metcalf, Linda Trichter & Simon, Tobin—*Writing the Mind Alive: The Proprioceptive Method for Finding Your Authentic Voice*

Moon, Janell—*Stirring the Waters: Writing to Find Your Spirit*

Yudkin, Marcia—*Writing Articles About the World Around You*

Zinsser, William—*On Writing Well*

Additional books on writing are listed in:

The Write Spot to Jumpstart Your Writing: Discoveries

The Write Spot: Memories

The Write Spot: Writing as a Path to Healing

Acknowledgments

It's easy. Just sit down and write. Write what you know. Write what you don't know. Just Write. It's so easy.

Yeah, right!

Maybe writing is easy for some, but the revision process can be challenging, just like our year 2020, filled with surprises and wishes for something better. Are writers ever satisfied with their finished pieces?

They are if they have an amazing community, like the writing village I'm delighted to be a part of.

"A village is a perfect place to live if you are in search of harmony with nature." I read that while searching for the definition of village. A writing village was the ideal place to produce this anthology, especially in 2020, when many felt isolated.

Thank you to The Write Spot Villagers for helping to create this compilation of excellent stories, which will hopefully add to the harmony and quality of life for readers.

My immense gratitude goes to the participating writers for your willingness to go the distance, for staying with the revising process, transforming first thoughts into polished products. *The Write Spot: Musings and Ravings From a Pandemic Year* would not have happened without you.

Thank you for your trust in me and in the process. In spite of a paralyzing pandemic, we did it!

I raise my glass to proofreaders M.A. Dooley, Karen Ely, Kathy Guthormsen, and Nick Valdez. I bow to you and your discerning abilities to spot elusive typos. You deserve gold stars for pointing out confusing places that, if not caught, would cause raised eyebrow and exclamations of "uh-oh."

Thank you, Diane McKay. I appreciate your help with making the freewrite section clear and orderly.

A carpetbag full of appreciation to Brenda Bellinger, my life saver and sanity saver, for making my writing sparkle. You look over my writing as carefully as tucking in a newborn. You are my Mary Poppins.

My admiration to Brenda Bellinger and Sandra Anfang for musings and confirmation about the title, demonstrating the importance of collaboration and supporting one another.

Reams of thanks to Jo-Anne Rosen, my mentor and formatting artist, who has an impressive ability to transform a word document into something precious and beautiful to hold. Your work is art.

About Marlene

I loved my childhood in the Mission District where I lived with my mother, two younger sisters, my part-time father, and his parents. Friday nights, I would take candy orders and venture to the corner grocery store for five-cent Snickers, Milky Ways, the chewy Look, and my mother's favorite, Uno. I was really taking a risk if I left our flat before the streetlights came on. In the dusky twilight I had to cross four lanes of traffic where cars raced to make the green light at the next corner. I'm lucky to be alive, after playing dodgeball with speeding vehicles.

Even though it wasn't safe to walk around at night, I did anyway and yes, I was accosted twice and robbed a couple of times . . . an element of living in a neighborhood where adrenaline factored in as part of life's adventures.

In second grade, I lived in Santa Clara with my parents and younger sister. When I missed the yellow school bus, I had to go into stealth mode to cross a walnut orchard to get to school, staying ahead of the angry farmer.

Later, I survived adventures vicariously through books, especially the Wizard of Oz series and Nancy Drew, a heroine I drew inspiration from, always looking for clues to life's mysteries.

Every Saturday when I was eleven years old, I walked five blocks from our flat on So. Van Ness Ave. to the public library on Bartlett St. Each week I brought home an armload of books that I consumed like ice cream, scooping up characters, plots, scenes, and dialogue. Like ice cream, the sweetness of the stories lingered, the chill of mysteries resolved after the denouement and the finale: the satisfaction of ideas swirling in my head.

I didn't know the word denouement then. That came later, when I read books about writing and took writing classes and workshops.

After so much book learning and workshop taking, I started writing with the idea of being published. That scary thought was eased by kindred souls I met in workshops and writing groups. Family and friends cheered me on.

Although deep down I always knew I was a writer, it took my dear friend, Pat Tyler, nudging me to enter a contest which led to my story being published, giving me the strength to seriously pursue writing for publication.

I met my future husband when I was seventeen. I went on a few ocean-going adventures with him and his family on the schooner they built (described in *The Write Spot to Jumpstart Your Writing: Discoveries*). Adrenaline on the high seas.

Fortunately, there wasn't much drama raising three children on our small plot of land in rural Petaluma, just the normal ups-and-downs of parenting.

And now, my adrenaline rush happens when I'm typing as fast as I can to meet a writing deadline.

My writing journey continues to unfold with Writers Forum, a literary series that I host on the Zoom platform.

Information about Writers Forum can be found on my website: www.TheWriteSpot.us

You are welcome to join our Facebook Writers Forum group: https://www.facebook.com/JumpstartYourWriting/

I hope to see you at a writing event, in person and online.